Mercadet
A Comedy In Three Acts

by
Honore De Balzac

Mercadet
A Comedy In Three Acts
by Honore De Balzac

Copyright © 2024

All Rights reserved.

No part of this publication may be reproduced, stored in a retrieval system, or transmitted in any form or by any means, electronic, mechanical, photocopying or Otherwise, without the written permission of the publisher.
The author/editor asserts the moral right to be identified as the author/editor of this work.

ISBN: 978-93-61152-47-4

Published by
DOUBLE 9 BOOKS
2/13-B, Ansari Road
Daryaganj, New Delhi – 110002
info@double9books.com
www.double9books.com
Tel. 011-40042856

This book is under public domain

ABOUT THE AUTHOR

French dramatist and writer Honore de Balzac (1799–1850) was well-known for his important contributions to 19th-century literature. Frenchman Balzac was born in Tours. His literary career started with some small achievements, but he gained global recognition with his ambitious undertaking, "La Comedie Humaine." Beginning in the 1830s, this vast anthology of books and stories sought to present a thorough and accurate picture of French society. Thorough observation, intricate characterizations, and a dedication to capturing the complexity of human nature define Balzac's writing style. His paintings frequently portrayed a diverse cast of persons from different socioeconomic backgrounds and examined the effects of social and economic factors on individuals. Balzac was taken to a wet nurse as a child; the following year, he was joined by his sister Laure, and they lived away from home for four years. (Although Genevan philosopher Jean-Jacques Rousseau's popular book Emile persuaded many mothers at the time to breastfeed their own children, sending babies to wet nurses remained common among the middle and upper classes.) When the Balzac children returned home, they were kept at a remove from their parents, which had a tremendous impact on the future novelist. His 1835 novel Le Lys dans la vallee portrays a nasty governess named Miss Caroline, who is based on his own caregiver.

CONTENTS

ACT I
    SCENE FIRST 7

    SCENE SECOND 10

    SCENE THIRD 11

    SCENE FOURTH 12

    SCENE FIFTH... 14

    SCENE SIXTH 18

    SCENE SEVENTH 23

    SCENE EIGHTH 28

    SCENE NINTH 30

    SCENE TENTH 31

    SCENE ELEVENTH 33

    SCENE TWELFTH 39

    SCENE THIRTEENTH 44

    SCENE FOURTEENTH 45

ACT II
    SCENE FIRST 46

    SCENE SECOND 47

    SCENE THIRD 54

    SCENE FOURTH 57

    SCENE FIFTH... 62

 SCENE SIXTH 68
 SCENE SEVENTH 70
 SCENE EIGHTH 73
 SCENE NINTH 79

ACT III
 SCENE FIRST 82
 SCENE SECOND 84
 SCENE THIRD 87
 SCENE FOURTH 92
 SCENE FIFTH... 95
 SCENE SIXTH 96
 SCENE SEVENTH 101
 SCENE EIGHTH 104
 SCENE NINTH 105
 SCENE TENTH 107
 SCENE ELEVENTH... 109
 SCENE TWELFTH 113
 SCENE THIRTEENTH 116
 SCENE FOURTEENTH 118

ACT I

SCENE FIRST

(A drawing-room. A door in the centre. Side doors. At the front, to the left, a mantel-piece with a mirror. To the right, a window, and next it a writing-table. Armchairs.)

Justin, Virginie and Therese

Justin (finishing dusting the room) Yes, my dears, he finds it very hard to swim; he is certain to drown, poor M. Mercadet.

Virginie (her basket on her arm)

Honestly, do you think that?

Justin He is ruined! And although there is much fat to be stewed from a master while he is financially embarrassed, you must not forget that he owes us a year's wages, and we had better get ourselves discharged.

Therese Some masters are so frightfully stubborn! I spoke to the mistress disrespectfully two or three times, and she pretended not to hear me.

Virginie Ah! I have been at service in many middle-class houses; but I have never seen one like this! I am going to leave my stove, and become an actress in some theatre.

Justin

All of us here are nothing but actors in a theatre.

Virginie Yes, indeed, sometimes one has to put on an air of astonishment, as if just fallen from the moon, when a creditor appears: "Didn't you know it, sir?"—"No."—"M. Mercadet has gone to Lyons."—"Ah! He is away?" —"Yes, his prospects are most brilliant; he has discovered some coal-mines."—"Ah! So much the better! When does he return?"—"I do not know." Sometimes I put on an expression as if I had lost the dearest friend I had in the world.

Justin (aside)

That would be her money.

Virginie (pretending to cry) "Monsieur and mademoiselle are in the greatest distress. It seems that we are going to lose poor Madame Mercadet. They have taken her away to the waters! Ah!"

Therese And then, there are some creditors who are actual brutes! They speak to you as if you were the masters!

Virginie There's an end of it. I ask them for their bill and tell them I am going to settle. But now, the tradesmen refuse to give anything without the money! And you may be sure that I am not going to lend any of mine.

Justin

Let us demand our wages.

Virginie and Therese

Yes, let us demand our wages.

Virginie Who are middle-class people? Middle-class people are those who spend a great deal on their kitchen—

Justin

Who are devoted to their servants—

Virginie And who leave them a pension. That is how middle-class people ought to behave to their servants.

Therese The lady of Picardy speaks well. But all the same, I pity mademoiselle and young Minard, her suitor.

Justin M. Mercadet is not going to give his daughter to a miserable bookkeeper who earns no more than eighteen hundred francs a year; he has better views for her than that.

Therese and Virginie

Who is the man he thinks of?

Justin

Yesterday two fine young gentlemen came here in a carriage, and their groom told old Gruneau that one of them was going to marry Mlle. Mercadet.

Virginie You don't mean to say so! Are those gentlemen in yellow gloves, with fine flowered waistcoats, going to marry mademoiselle?

Justin

Not both of them, lady of Picardy.

Virginie The panels of their carriage shone like satin. Their horse had rosettes here. (She points to her ears.) It was held by a boy of eight, fair, with frizzed hair and top boots. He looked as sly as a mouse—a very Cupid, though he swore like a trooper. His master is as fine as a picture, with a big diamond in his scarf. It ain't possible that a handsome young man who owns such a turnout as that is going to be the husband of Mlle. Mercadet? I can't believe it.

Justin You don't know M. Mercadet! I, who have been in his house for the last six years, and have seen him since his troubles fighting with his creditors, can believe him capable of anything, even of growing rich; sometimes I say to myself he is utterly ruined! Yellow auction placards flame at his door. He receives reams of stamped creditor's notices, which I sell by the pound for waste paper without being noticed. But presto! Up he bobs again. He is triumphant. And what devices he has! There is a new one every day! First of all, it is a scheme for wooden pavements—then it is dukedoms, ponds, mills. I don't know where the leakage is in his cash box; he finds it so hard to fill; for it empties itself as easily as a drained wine-glass! And always crowds of creditors! How well he turns them away! Sometimes I have seen them come with the intention of carrying off everything and throwing him into prison. But when he talks to them they end by being the best of friends, and part with cordial handshakes! There are some men who can tame jackals and lions. That's not a circumstance; M. Mercadet can tame creditors!

Therese

One of them is not quite so easily managed; and that is M. Pierquin.

Justin

He is a tiger who feeds on bankrupts. And to think of poor old

Violette!

Virginie He is both creditor and beggar—I always feel inclined to give him a plate of soup.

Justin

And Goulard!

Therese

A bill discounter who would like very much to—to discount me.

Virginie (amid a general laugh)

I hear madame coming.

Justin Let us keep a civil tongue in our heads, and we shall learn something about the marriage.

SCENE SECOND

The same persons and Mme. Mercadet.

Mme. Mercadet

Justin, have you executed the commissions I gave you?

Justin Yes, madame, but they refused to deliver the dresses, the hats, and indeed all the things you ordered until—

Virginie And I also have to inform madame that the tradesmen are no longer willing—

Mme. Mercadet

I understand.

Justin The creditors are the cause of the whole trouble. I wish I knew how to get even with them.

Mme. Mercadet

The best way to do so would be to pay them.

Justin

They would be mightily surprised.

Mme. Mercadet It is useless to conceal from you the excessive anxiety which I suffer over the condition of my husband's affairs. We shall doubtless be in need of your discretion—for we can depend upon you, can we not?

All

You need not mention it, madame.

Virginie

We were just saying, what excellent employers we had.

Therese

And that we would go through fire and water for you!

Justin

We were saying—

(Mercadet appears unnoticed.)

Mme. Mercadet Thank you all, you are good creatures. (Mercadet shrugs his shoulders.) Your master needs only time, he has so many schemes in his head!—a rich suitor has offered himself for Mlle. Julie, and if—

SCENE THIRD

The same persons and Mercadet.

Mercadet (interrupting his wife) My dearest! (The servants draw back a little. In a low voice to madame) And so this is how you speak to the servants! To-morrow they laugh at us. (To Justin) Justin, go at once to M. Verdelin's house, and ask him to come here, as I want to speak to him about a piece of business that will not admit of delay. Assume an air of mystery, for I must have him come. You, Therese, go to the tradesmen of Madame de Mercadet, and tell them, sharply, that they must send the things that have been ordered.—They will be paid for—yes—and cash, too—go at once. (Justin and Therese start.) Ah!—(They stop.) If—these people come to the house again, ask them to enter. (Mme. Mercadet takes a seat.)

Justin

These—these people?—

Therese and Virginie

These people? Eh!

Mercadet

Yes, these people—these creditors of mine!—

Mme. Mercadet

How is this, my dear?

Mercadet (taking a seat opposite his wife)

I am weary of solitude—I want their society. (To Justin and Therese)

That will do.

(Justin and Therese leave the room.)

SCENE FOURTH

Mercadet, Mme. Mercadet and Virginie.

Mercadet (to Virginie)

Has madame given you any orders?

Virginie

No, sir, and besides the tradespeople—

Mercadet I hope you will do yourself credit to-day. We are going to have four people to dinner—Verdelin and his wife, M. de Mericourt and M. de la Brive—so there will be seven of us. Such dinners are the glory of great cooks! You must have a fine fish after the soup, then two entrees, very delicately cooked—

Virginie

But, sir, the trades—

Mercadet For the second course—ah, the second course ought to be at once rich and brilliant, yet solid. The second course—

Virginie

But the tradespeople—

Mercadet Nonsense! You annoy me—To talk about tradespeople on the day when my daughter and her intended are to meet!

Virginie

They won't supply anything.

Mercadet What have we got to do with tradespeople that won't take our trade? We must get others. You must go to their competitors, you must give them my custom, and they will tip you for it.

Virginie

And how shall I pay those that I am giving up?

Mercadet

Don't worry yourself about that,—it is my business.

Virginie

But if they ask me to pay them—

Mercadet (aside, rising to his feet) That girl has money of her own. (Aloud) Virginie, in these days, credit is the sole wealth of the government. My tradespeople misunderstand the laws of their country, they will show themselves unconstitutional and utter radicals, unless they leave me alone.— Don't you trouble your head about people who raise an insurrection against the vital principles of all rightly constituted states! What you have got to attend to, is dinner,—that is your duty, and I hope that on this occasion you will show yourself to be what you are, a first-class cook! And if Mme. Mercadet, when she settles with you on the day after my daughter's wedding, finds that she owes you anything, I will hold myself liable for it all.

Virginie (hesitating)

Sir—

Mercadet Now go about your business. I give you here an opportunity of gaining an interest of ten per cent every six months!—and that is better than the savings banks will do for you.

Virginie

That it is; they only give four per cent a year!

Mercadet (whispering to his wife) What did I tell you!—(To Virginie) How can you run the risk of putting your money into the hands of strangers—You are quite clever enough to invest it yourself, and here your little nest-egg will remain in your own possession.

Virginie Ten per cent every six months!—I suppose that madame will give me the particulars with regard to the second course. I must start to work on it. (Exit.)

SCENE FIFTH

Mercadet and Mme. Mercadet

Mercadet (watching Virginie as she goes out) That girl has a thousand crowns of our good money in the savings bank, so that we needn't worry about the kitchen for awhile.

Mme. Mercadet

Ah! sir, how can you stoop to such a thing as this?

Mercadet Madame, these are mere petty details; don't bother about the means to an end. You, a little time ago, were trying to control your servants by kindness, but it is necessary to command and compel them, and to do it briefly, like Napoleon.

Mme. Mercadet

How can you order them when you don't pay them?

Mercadet

You must pay them by a bluff.

Mme. Mercadet

Sometimes you can obtain by affection what is not attainable by—

Mercadet By affection! Ah! Little do you know the age in which we live—To-day, madame, wealth is everything, family is nothing; there are no families, but only individuals! The future of each one is to be determined by the public funds. A young girl when she needs a dowry no longer appeals to her family, but to a syndicate. The income of the King of England comes from an insurance company. The wife depends for funds, not upon her husband, but upon the savings bank!—Debts are paid, not to creditors, but to the country, through an agency, which manages a sort of slave-trade in white people! All our duties are arranged by coupons—The servants which we exchange for them are no longer attached to their masters, but if you hold their money they will be devoted to you.

Mme. Mercadet Oh, sir, you who are so honorable, so upright, sometimes say things to me which—

Mercadet And what is said may also be done, that is what you mean, isn't it? Undoubtedly I would do anything to save myself, for (he pulls out a five-franc piece) this represents modern honor. Do you know why the dramas that have criminals for their heroes are so popular? It is because all the audience flatter themselves and say, "at any rate, I am much better than that fellow!"

Mme. Mercadet

My dear!

Mercadet For my part I have an excuse, for I am bearing the burden of my partner's crime—of that fellow Godeau, who absconded, carrying with him the cash box of our house!—And besides that, what disgrace is it to be in debt? What man is there who does not owe his father his existence? He can never repay that debt. The earth is constantly bankrupt to the sun. Life, madame, is a perpetual loan! Am I not superior to my creditors? I have their money, when they can only expect mine. I do not ask anything of them, and yet they are constantly importuning me.—A man who does not owe anything is not thought about by any one, while my creditors take a keen interest in me.

Mme. Mercadet They take rather too much! To owe and to pay is well enough—but to borrow without any prospect of returning—

Mercadet You feel a great deal of compassion for my creditors, but our indebtedness to them springs from—

Mme. Mercadet

Their confidence in us, sir.

Mercadet No, but from their greed of gain! The speculator and the broker are one and the same—each of them aims at sudden wealth. I have done a favor to all my creditors, and they all expect to get something out of me! I should be most unhappy but for the secret consciousness I have that they are selfish and avaricious—so that you will see in a few moments how I will make each of them play out his little comedy. (He sits down.)

Mme. Mercadet

You have actually ordered them to be admitted?

Mercadet That I may meet them as I ought to!—(taking her hand.) I am at the end of my resources; the time has come for a master-stroke, and Julie must come to our assistance.

Mme. Mercadet

What, my daughter!

Mercadet My creditors are pressing me, and harassing me. I must manage to make a brilliant match for Julie. This will dazzle them; they will give me more time. But in order that this brilliant marriage may take place, these gentlemen must give me more money.

Mme. Mercadet

They give you more money!

Mercadet Isn't there need of it for the dresses which they are sending to you, and for the trousseau which I am giving? And a suitable trousseau to go with the dowry of two hundred thousand francs, will cost fifteen thousand.

Mme. Mercadet

But you are utterly unable to give such a dowry.

Mercadet (rising) All the more reason why I should give the trousseau. Now this is what we stand in need of: twelve or fifteen thousand francs for the trousseau, and a thousand crowns to pay the tradesmen and to prevent any appearance of straitened circumstances in our house, when M. de la Brive arrives.

Mme. Mercadet

How can you count on your creditors for that?

Mercadet Don't they now belong to the family? Can you find any relation who is as anxious as they are to see me wealthy and rich? Relations are always a little envious of the happiness of the wealth which comes to us; the creditor's joy alone is sincere. If I were to die, I should have at my funeral more creditors than relations, and while the latter carried their mourning in their hearts or on their heads, the former would carry it in their ledgers and purses. It is here that my departure would leave a genuine void! The heart forgets, and crape disappears at the end of a year, but the account which is unpaid is ineffaceable, and the void remains eternally unfilled.

Mme. Mercadet My dear, I know the people to whom you are indebted, and I am quite certain that you will obtain nothing from them.

Mercadet I shall obtain both time and money from them, rest assured of that. (Mme. Mercadet is perturbed.) Don't you see, my dear, that creditors when once they have opened their purses are like gamblers who continue to stake their money in order to recover their first losses? (Growing excited.) Yes! they are inexhaustible gold mines! If a man has no father to leave him a fortune, he finds his creditors are so many indefatigable uncles.

Justin (entering)

M. Goulard wishes to know if it is true that you desire to see him?

Mercadet (to his wife) My message astounded him. (To Justin) Beg him to come in. (Justin goes out.) Goulard! The most intractable of them all!—who has three bailiffs in his employ. But fortunately he is a greedy though timid speculator who engages in the most risky affairs and trembles all the time they are being conducted.

Justin (announcing)

M. Goulard!

(Exit Justin.)

SCENE SIXTH

The same persons and Goulard.

Goulard (in anger)

Ah! you can be found, sir, when you want to be!

Mme. Mercadet (aside to her husband)

My dear, how angry he seems!

Mercadet (making a sign that she should be calm)

This is one of my creditors, my dear.

Goulard

Yes, and I sha'n't leave this house until you pay me.

Mercadet (aside) You sha'n't leave this house until you give me some money—(Aloud) Ah! you have persecuted me most unkindly—me, a man with whom you have had such extensive dealings!

Goulard

Dealings which have not always been to my advantage.

Mercadet All the more credit to you, for if advantage were the sole results of business, everybody would become a money-lender.

Goulard I hope you haven't asked me to come here, in order to show me how clever you are! I know that you are cleverer than I am, for you have got over me in money matters.

Mercadet Well, money matters have some importance. (To his wife) Yes, yes, you see in this man one who has hunted me as if I were a hare. Come, come, Goulard, admit it, you have behaved badly. Anybody but myself would have taken vengeance on you—for of course I could cause you to lose a considerable sum of money.

Goulard So you could, if you didn't pay me; but you shall pay me—your obligations are now in the hands of the law.

Mme. Mercadet

Of the law?

Mercadet Of the law! You are losing your senses, you don't know what you are doing, you are ruining us both—yourself and me—at the same time.

Goulard (anxiously)

How?—You—that of course is possible—but—but—me?

Mercadet

Both of us, I tell you! Quick, sit down there—write—write—!

Goulard (mechanically taking his pen)

Write—write what?

Mercadet Write to Delannoy that he must make them stay the proceedings, and give me the thousand crowns which I absolutely need.

Goulard (throwing down the pen)

That is very likely, indeed!

Mercadet

You hesitate, and, when I am on the eve of marrying my daughter to a

man immensely wealthy—that is the time you choose to cause my arrest.

And by that means you are killing both your capital and interest!

Goulard

Ah! you are going to marry your daughter—

Mercadet To the Comte de la Brive; he possesses as many thousand francs as he is years old!

Goulard Then if he is up in years, there is reason for giving you some delay. But the thousand crowns—the thousand crowns—never.—I am quite decided on that point. I will give you nothing, neither delay nor—I must go now—

Mercadet (with energy) Very well! You can go if you like, you ungrateful fellow!—But don't forget that I have done my best to save you.

Goulard (turning back)

Me?—To save me—from what?

Mercadet (aside)

I have him now. (Aloud) From what?—From the most complete ruin.

Goulard

Ruin? It is impossible.

Mercadet (taking a seat) What is the matter with you? You, a man of intelligence, of ability—a strong man, and yet you cause me all this trouble! You came here and I felt absolutely enraged against you—not because I was your friend, I confess it, but through selfishness. I look upon our interests as identical. I said to myself: I owe him so much that he is sure to give me his assistance when I have such a grand chance—like the one at this moment! And you are going to let out the whole business and to lose everything for the sake of a paltry sum! Everything! You are perhaps right in refusing me the thousand crowns—It is better, perhaps, to bury them in your coffers with the rest. All right! Send me to prison! Then, when all is gone, you'll have to look somewhere else for a friend!

Goulard (in a tone of self-reproach)

Mercadet!—my dear Mercadet!—But is it actually true?

Mercadet (rising from his seat)

Is it true? (to his wife) You would not believe he was so stupid. (To Goulard) She has ended by becoming a daring speculator. (To his wife) I may tell you, my dear, that Goulard is going to invest a large sum in our great enterprise.

Mme. Mercadet (ashamed)

Sir!

Mercadet

What a misfortune it will be if it does not turn out well.

Goulard

Mercadet!—Are you talking about the Basse-Indre mines?

Mercadet Of course I am. (Aside) Ah! You have some of the Basse-Indre stock, I see.

Goulard

But the investment seems to me first-class.

Mercadet

First-class—Yes, for those who sold out yesterday.

Goulard

Have any stockholders sold out?

Mercadet

Yes, privately.

Goulard

Good-bye. Thanks, Mercadet; madame, accept my respects.

Mercadet (stopping him)

Goulard!

Goulard

Eh?

Mercadet

What about this note to Delannoy?

Goulard

I will speak to him about the postponement—

Mercadet No; write to him; and in the meantime I will find some one who will buy your stock.

Goulard (sitting down)

All my Basse-Indre? (He takes up a pen.)

Mercadet (aside)

Here you see the honest man, ever ready to rob his neighbor. (Aloud)

Very well, write—ordering a postponement of three months.

Goulard (writing)

Three months! There you have it.

Mercadet The man I allude to, who buys in secret for fear of causing a rise, wants to get three hundred shares; do you happen to have three hundred?

Goulard

I have three hundred and fifty.

Mercadet Fifty more! Never mind! He'll take them all. (Examining what Goulard has written.) Have you mentioned the thousand crowns?

Goulard

And what is your friend's name?

Mercadet

His name? You haven't mentioned?—

Goulard

His name!

Mercadet

The thousand crowns.

Goulard

What a devil of a man he is! (He writes.) There, you have it!

Mercadet

His name is Pierquin.

Goulard (rising)

Pierquin.

Mercadet He at least is the nominal buyer.—Go to your house and I will send him to you; it is never a good thing to run after a purchaser.

Goulard Never!—You have saved my life. Good-bye, my friend. Madame, accept my prayers for the happiness of your daughter. (Exit.)

Mercadet

One of them captured! Now watch me get the others!

SCENE SEVENTH

Mme. Mercadet, Mercadet, then Julie.

Mme. Mercadet Is there any truth in what you just now said? I could not quite follow you.

Mercadet It is to the interest of my friend Verdelin to cause a panic in Basse- Indre stock; this stock has been for a long time very risky and has suddenly become of first-class value, through the discovery of certain beds of mineral, which are known only to those on the inside. — Ah! If I could but invest a thousand crowns in it my fortune would be made. But, of course, our main object at present is the marriage of Julie.

Mme. Mercadet

You are well acquainted with M. de la Brive, are you not?

Mercadet I have dined with him. He has a charming apartment, fine plate, a silver dessert service, bearing his arms, so that it could not have been borrowed. Our daughter is going to make a fine match, and he— when either one of a married couple is happy, it is all right.

(Julie enters.)

Mme. Mercadet Here comes our daughter. Julie, your father and I have something to say to you on a subject which is always agreeable to a young girl.

Julie

M. Minard has then spoken to you, father?

Mercadet M. Minard! Did you expect, madame, to find a M. Minard reigning in the heart of your daughter? Is not this M. Minard that under clerk of mine?

Julie

Yes, papa.

Mercadet

Do you love him?

Julie

Yes, papa.

Mercadet

But besides loving, it is necessary for a person to be loved.

Mme. Mercadet

Does he love you?

Julie

Yes, mamma!

Mercadet Yes, papa; yes, mamma; why don't you say mammy and daddy?—As soon as daughters have passed their majority they begin to talk as if they were just weaned. Be polite enough to address your mother as madame.

Julie

Yes, monsieur.

Mercadet Oh! you may address me as papa. I sha'n't be annoyed at that. What proof have you that he loves you?

Julie

The best proof of all; he wishes to marry me.

Mercadet It is quite true, as has been said, that young girls, like little children, have answers ready enough to knock one silly. Let me tell you, mademoiselle, that a clerk with a salary of eighteen hundred francs does not know how to love. He hasn't got the time, he has to work too hard—

Mme. Mercadet

But, unhappy child—

Mercadet Ah! A lucky thought strikes me! Let me talk to her. Julie, listen to me. I will marry you to Minard. (Julie smiles with delight.) Now, look here, you haven't got a single sou, and you know it; what is going to become of you a week after your marriage? Have you thought about that?

Julie

Yes, papa—

Mme. Mercadet (with sympathy, to her husband)

The poor child is mad.

Mercadet Yes, she is in love. (To Julie) Tell me all about it, Julie. I am not now your father, but your confidant; I am listening.

Julie

After our marriage we will still love each other.

Mercadet

But will Cupid shoot you bank coupons at the end of his arrows?

Julie Father, we shall lodge in a small apartment, at the extremity of the Faubourg, on the fourth story, if necessary!—And if it can't be helped, I will be his house-maid. Oh! I will take an immense delight in the care of the household, for I shall know that it will all be done for him. I will work for him, while he is working for me. I will spare him every anxiety, and he will never know how straitened we are. Our home will be spotlessly clean, even elegant—You shall see! Elegance depends upon such little things; it springs from the soul, and happiness is at once the cause and the effect of it. I can earn enough from my painting to cost him nothing and even to contribute to the expenses of our living. Moreover, love will help us to pass through the days of hardship. Adolphe has ambition, like all those who are of lofty soul, and these are the successful men—

Mercadet Success is within reach of the bachelor, but, when a man is married, he exhausts himself in meeting his expenses, and runs after a thousand franc bill as a dog runs after a carriage.

Julie But, papa, Adolphe has strength of will, united with such capacity that I feel sure I shall see him some day a Minister, perhaps—

Mercadet In these days, who is there that does not indulge more or less the hope of being a minister? When a man leaves college he thinks himself a great poet, or a great orator! Do you know what your Adolphe will really become?—Why, the father of several children, who will utterly disarrange your plans of work and economy, who will end by landing his excellency in the debtor's prison, and who will plunge you into the most frightful poverty. What you have related to me is the romance and not the reality of life.

Mme. Mercadet

Daughter, there can be nothing serious in this love of yours.

Julie

It is a love to which both of us are willing to sacrifice everything.

Mercadet

I suppose that your friend Adolphe thinks that we are rich?

Julie

He has never spoken to me about money.

Mercadet Just so. I can quite understand it. (To Julie) Julie, write to him at once, telling him to come to me.

Julie (kissing him)

Dear papa!

Mercadet And you must marry M. de la Brive. Instead of living on a fourth floor in a suburb, you will have a fine house in the Chaussee-d'Antin, and, if you are not the wife of a Minister, you perhaps will be the wife of a peer of France. I am sorry, my daughter, that I have no more to offer you. Remember, you can have no choice in the matter, for M. Minard is going to give you up.

Julie

Oh! he will never do that, papa. He will win your heart—

Mme. Mercadet

My dear, suppose he loves her?

Mercadet

He is deceiving her—

Julie

I shouldn't mind being always deceived in that way.

(A bell is heard without.)

Mme. Mercadet

Some one is ringing, and we have no one to open the door.

Mercadet

That is all right. Let them ring.

Mme. Mercadet

I am all the time thinking that Godeau may return.

Mercadet

After eight years without any news, you are still expecting Godeau! You seem to me like those old soldiers who are waiting for the return of Napoleon.

Mme. Mercadet

They are ringing again.

Mercadet Julie, go and see who it is, and tell them that your mother and I have gone out. If any one is shameless enough to disbelieve a young girl—it must be a creditor—let him come in.

(Exit Julie.)

Mme. Mercadet This love she speaks of, and which, at least on her side, is sincere, disturbs me greatly.

Mercadet

You women are all too romantic.

Julie (returning)

It is M. Pierquin, papa.

Mercadet A creditor and usurer—a vile and violent soul, who humors me because he thinks me a man of resources; a wild beast only half-tamed yet cowed by my audacity. If I showed fear he would devour me. (Going to the door.) Come in, Pierquin, come in.

SCENE EIGHTH

The same persons and Pierquin.

Pierquin My congratulations to you all. I hear that you are making a grand marriage for your daughter. Mademoiselle is to marry a millionaire; the report has already gone abroad.

Mercadet A millionaire?—No, he has only nine hundred thousand francs, at the most.

Pierquin This magnificent prospect will induce a lot of people to give you time. They are becoming devilishly tired of your talk about Godeau's return. And I myself—

Mercadet

Were you thinking about having me arrested?

Julie

Arrested!

Mme. Mercadet (to Pierquin)

Ah! sir.

Pierquin Now listen to me, you have had two years, and I never before let a bond go over so long; but this marriage is a glorious invention and—

Mme. Mercadet

An invention!

Mercadet

Sir, my future son-in-law, M. de la Brive, is a young man—

Pierquin So that there is a real young man in the case? How much are you going to pay the young man?

Mme. Mercadet

Oh!

Mercadet (checking his wife by a sign) No more of this insolence! Otherwise, my dear sir, I shall be forced to demand a settlement of our accounts—and, my dear M. Pierquin, you will lose a good deal of the price at which you sold your money to me. And at the rate of interest you charge, I shall cost you more than the value of a farm in Bauce.

Pierquin

Sir—

Mercadet (haughtily) Sir, I shall soon be so rich that I will not endure to be twitted by any one—not even by a creditor.

Pierquin

But—

Mercadet Not a word—or I will pay you! Come into my private room and we will settle the business about which I asked you to come.

Pierquin

I am at your service, sir. (Aside) What a devil of a man!

(Pierquin and Mercadet bow to the ladies and enter Mercadet's room.)

Mercadet (following Pierquin; aside to his wife)

The wild beast is tamed. I'll get this one, too.

SCENE NINTH

Mme. Mercadet, Julie, and later, Servants.

Julie

O mamma! I cannot marry this M. de la Brive!

Mme. Mercadet

But he is rich, you know.

Julie

But I prefer happiness and poverty, to unhappiness and wealth.

Mme. Mercadet My child, happiness is impossible in poverty, while there is no misfortune that wealth cannot alleviate.

Julie

How can you say such sad words to me?

Mme. Mercadet Children should learn a lesson from the experience of parents. We are at present having a very bitter taste of life's vicissitudes. Take my advice, daughter, and marry wealth.

Justin (entering, followed by Therese and Virginie)

Madame, we have carried out the master's orders.

Virginie

My dinner will be ready.

Therese

And the tradesmen have consented.

Justin

As far as concerns M. Verdelin—

SCENE TENTH

The same persons and Mercadet (carrying a bundle of papers).

Mercadet

What did my friend Verdelin say?

Justin He will be here in a moment. He was just on his way here to bring some money to M. Bredif, the owner of this house.

Mercadet Bredif is a millionaire. Take care that Verdelin speaks to me before going up to him. How did you get on, Therese, with the milliners and dressmakers?

Therese Sir, as soon as I gave them a promise of payment, every one greeted me with smiles.

Mercadet

Very good. And shall we have a fine dinner, Virginie?

Virginie

You will compliment it, sir, when you eat it.

Mercadet

And the tradespeople?

Virginie

They will wait your time.

Mercadet

I shall settle with you all to-morrow. You can go now. (They go out.)

A man who has his servants with him is like a minister who has the press on his side!

Mme. Mercadet

And what of Pierquin?

Mercadet (showing the papers) All that I could extort from him is as follows.—He will give me time, and this negotiable paper in exchange for stock.—Also notes for forty-seven thousand francs, to be collected from a man named Michonnin, a gentleman broker, not considered very solvent, who may be a crook but has a very rich aunt at Bordeaux; M. de la Brive is from that district and I can learn from him if there is anything to be got out of it.

Mme. Mercadet

But the tradesmen will soon arrive.

Mercadet

I shall be here to receive them. Now leave me, leave me, my dears.

(Exeunt the two ladies.)

SCENE ELEVENTH

Mercadet, then Violette.

Mercadet (walking up and down) Yes, they will soon be here! And everything depends upon that somewhat slippery friendship of Verdelin—a man whose fortune I made! Ah! when a man has passed forty he learns that the world is peopled by the ungrateful—I do not know where all the benefactors have gone to. Verdelin and I have a high opinion of each other. He owes me gratitude, I owe him money, and neither of us pays the other. And now, in order to arrange the marriage of Julie, my business is to find a thousand crowns in a pocket which pretends to be empty—to find entrance into a heart in order to find entrance into a cash-box! What an undertaking! Only women can do such things, and with men who are in love with them.

Justin (without)

Yes, he is in.

Mercadet

It is he. (Violette appears.) Ah! my friend! It is dear old Violette!

Violette This is the eleventh call within a week, my dear M. Mercadet, and my actual necessity has driven me to wait for you three hours in the street; I thought the truth was told me when I was assured that you were in the country. But I came to-day—

Mercadet

Ah! Violette, old fellow, we are both hard up!

Violette Humph! I don't think so. For my part, I've pledged everything I could put in the pawn-shop.

Mercadet

So have we.

Violette I have never reproached you with my ruin, for I believe it is your intention to enrich me, as well as yourself; but still, fine words butter no parsnips, and I am come to implore you to give me a small sum on account, and by so doing you will save the lives of a whole family.

Mercadet My dear old Violette, you grieve me deeply! Be reasonable and I will share with you. (In a low voice) We have scarcely a hundred francs in the house, and even that is my daughter's money.

Violette

Is it possible! You, Mercadet, whom I have known so rich?

Mercadet

I conceal nothing from you.

Violette

Unfortunate people owe it to each other to speak the truth.

Mercadet Ah! If that were the only thing they owed how prompt would be the payment! But keep this as a secret, for I am on the point of making a good match for my daughter.

Violette I have two daughters, sir, and they work without hope of being married! In your present circumstances I cannot press you, but my wife and my daughters await my return in the deepest anxiety.

Mercadet

Stay a moment. I will give you sixty francs.

Violette Ah! my wife and my girls will bless you. (Aside, while Mercadet leaves the room for a moment.) The others who abuse him get nothing out of him, but by appealing to his pity, little by little I get back my money. (Chuckles and slaps his pocket.)

Mercadet (on the point of re-entering sees this action) The beggarly old miser! Sixty francs on account paid ten times makes six hundred francs. Come now, I have sown enough, it is time to reap the harvest. (Aloud) Take this.

Violette

Sixty francs in gold! It is a long time since I have seen such a sum.

Good-bye, we sha'n't forget to pray for the speedy marriage of Mlle.

Mercadet.

Mercadet Good-bye, dear old Violette. (Holding him by the hand.) Poor old man, when I look at you, I think myself rich—your misfortunes touch me deeply. And yesterday I thought I would soon be on the point of paying back to you not only the interest but the principal of what I owe you.

Violette (turning back)

Paying me back! In full!

Mercadet

It was a close shave.

Violette

What was?

Mercadet Imagine, my dear fellow, that there exists a most brilliant opportunity, a most magnificent speculation, the most sublime discovery— an affair which appeals to the interest of every one, which will draw upon all the exchanges, and for the realization of which a stupid banker has refused me the miserable sum of a thousand crowns— when there is more than a million in sight.

Violette

A million!

Mercadet Yes, a million, from the start. Afterwards no one can calculate where the rage for protective pavement will stop.

Violette

Pavement?

Mercadet

Protective pavement. A pavement on which no barricade can be raised.

Violette

Really?

Mercadet You see, that from henceforth all governments interested in the preservation of order will become our chief shareholders—Ministers, princes and kings will be our chief partners. Next come the gods of finance, the great bankers, those of independent income in commerce and speculation; even the socialists, seeing that their industry is ruined, will be forced to buy stocks for a living from me!

Violette

Yes, it is fine! It is grand!

Mercadet It is sublime and philanthropic! And to think I have been refused four thousand francs, wherewith to send out advertisements and launch my prospectus!

Violette

Four thousand francs! I thought it was only—

Mercadet Four thousand francs, no more! And I was to give away for the loan a half interest in the enterprise—that is to say a fortune! Ten fortunes!

Violette

Listen—I will see—I will speak to some one—

Mercadet Speak to no one! Keep it to yourself! The idea would at once be snatched up—or perhaps they wouldn't understand it so well as you have immediately done. These money dealers are so stupid. Besides, I am expecting Verdelin here—

Violette

Verdelin—but—we might perhaps—

Mercadet 'Twill be lucky for Verdelin, if he has the brains to risk six thousand francs in it.

Violette

But you said four thousand just now.

Mercadet

It was four thousand that they refused me, but I need six thousand! Six thousand francs, and Verdelin, whom I have already made a millionaire once, is likely to become so three, four, five times over! But he will deserve it, for he is a clever fellow, is Verdelin.

Violette

Mercadet, I will find you the money.

Mercadet No, no, don't think of it. Besides, he will be here in a moment, and if I am to send him away without concluding the business with him, it will be necessary to have it settled with some one else before Verdelin comes—and, as that is impossible—good-bye—and good luck—I shall certainly be able to pay you your thirty thousand francs.

Violette

But say—why couldn't I—?

Mme. Mercadet (entering)

M. Verdelin has come, my dear.

Mercadet (aside) Good, good! (Aloud) Just detain him a minute. (Mme. Mercadet goes out.) Well, good-bye, dear old Violette—

Violette (pulling out a greasy pocketbook) Wait a moment—here, I have the money with me—and will give it you beforehand.

Mercadet

You! Six thousand francs!

Violette

A friend asked me to invest it for him, and—

Mercadet And you couldn't find a better opening. We'll sign the contract presently! (He takes the bills.) This closes the deal—and so much the worse for Verdelin—he has missed a gold mine!

Violette

Well, I'll see you later.

Mercadet

Yes—see you later! You can get out through my study.

(Mercadet shows Violette the way out. Mme. Mercadet enters.)

Mme. Mercadet

Mercadet!

Mercadet (reappearing)

Ah! my dear! I am an unfortunate man! I ought to blow my brains out.

Mme. Mercadet

Good heavens! What is the matter?

Mercadet The matter is that a moment ago I asked this sham bankrupt Violette for six thousand francs.

Mme. Mercadet

And he refused to give them to you?

Mercadet

On the contrary, he handed them over.

Mme. Mercadet

What, then, do you mean?

Mercadet I am an unlucky man, as I told you, because he gave them so quickly that I could have gotten ten thousand if I had only known it.

Mme. Mercadet What a man you are! I suppose you know that Verdelin is waiting for you.

Mercadet Beg him to come in. At last I have Julie's trousseau; and we now need only enough money for your dresses and for household expenses until the marriage. Send in Verdelin.

Mme. Mercadet

Yes, he is your friend, and of course you will gain your end with him.

(Exit Mme. Mercadet.)

Mercadet (alone) Yes, he is my friend! And he has all the pride that comes with fortune; but he has never had a Godeau (looking round to see if he is alone). After all, Godeau! I really believe that Godeau has brought me in more money than he has taken from me.

SCENE TWELFTH

Mercadet and Verdelin.

Verdelin Good-day, Mercadet. What is doing now? Tell me quickly for I was stopped here on my way up-stairs to Bredif's apartment.

Mercadet

Oh, he can wait! How is it that you are going to see a man like Bredif?

Verdelin (laughing) My dear friend, if people only visited those they esteem they would make no visits at all.

Mercadet (laughing and taking his hand)

A man wouldn't go even into his own house.

Verdelin

But tell me what you want with me?

Mercadet Your question is so sudden that it hasn't left me time to gild the pill.

Verdelin Oh! my old comrade. I have nothing, and I am frank to say that even if I had I could give you nothing. I have already lent you all that my means permit me to dispose of; I have never asked you for payment, for I am your friend as well as your creditor, and indeed, if my heart did not overflow in gratitude towards you, if I had not been a man different from ordinary men, the creditor would long ago have killed the man. I tell you everything has a limit in this world.

Mercadet

Friendship has a limit, that's certain; but not misfortune.

Verdelin If I were rich enough to save you altogether, to cancel your debt entirely, I would do so with all my heart, for I admire your courage. But you are bound to go under. Your last schemes, although cleverly projected, have collapsed. You have ruined your reputation, you are looked upon as a dangerous man. You have not known how to take advantage of the momentary success of your operations. When you are utterly beggared, you will always find bread at my house; but it is the duty of a friend to speak these plain truths.

Mercadet What would be the advantage of friendship unless it gave us the pleasure of finding ourselves in the right, and seeing a friend in the wrong—of being comfortable ourselves and seeing our friend in difficulties and of paying compliment to ourselves by saying disagreeable things to him? Is it true then that I am little thought of on 'Change?

Verdelin I do not say so much as that. No; you still pass for an honest man, but necessity is forcing you to adopt expedients—

Mercadet Which are not justified by the success which luckier men enjoy! Ah, success! How many outrageous things go to make up success. You'll learn that soon enough. Now, for instance, this morning I began to bear the market on the mines of Basse-Indre, in order that you may gain control of that enterprise before the favorable report of the engineers is published.

Verdelin Hush, Mercadet, can this be true? Ah! I see your genius there! (Puts his arm around him.)

Mercadet I say this in order that you may understand that I have no need of advice, or of moralizing,—merely of money. Alas! I do not ask any thing of you for myself, my dear friend, but I am about to make a marriage for my daughter, and here we are actually, although secretly, fallen into absolute destitution. We are in a house where poverty reigns under the appearance of luxury. The power of promises, and of credit, all is exhausted! And if I cannot pay in cash for certain necessary expenses, this marriage must be broken off. All I went here is a fortnight of opulence, just as all that you want is twenty-four hours of lying on the Exchange. Verdelin, this request will never be repeated, for I have only one daughter. Must I confess it to you? My wife and daughter are absolutely destitute of clothes! (Aside) He is hesitating.

Verdelin (aside) He has played me so many tricks that I really do not know whether his daughter is doing to be married or not. How can she marry?

Mercadet This very day I have to give a dinner to my future son-in-law, whom a mutual friend is introducing to us, and I haven't even my plate remaining in the house. It is—you know where it is—I not only need a thousand crowns, but I also hope that you will lend me your dinner service and come and dine here with your wife.

Verdelin A thousand crowns! Mercadet! No one has a thousand crowns to lend. One scarcely has them for himself; if he were to lend them whenever he was asked, he would never have them. (He retires to the fire-place.)

Mercadet (following him, aside) He will yet come to the scratch. (Aloud) Now look here, Verdelin, I love my wife and my daughter; these sentiments, my friend, are my sole consolation in the midst of my recent disasters; these women have been so gentle, so patient! I should like to see them placed beyond the reach of distress. Oh! It is on this point that my sufferings are most real! (They walk to the front of the stage arm in arm.) I have recently drunk the cup of bitterness, I have slipped upon my wooden pavement,—I organized a monopoly and others drained me of everything! But, believe me, this is nothing in comparison with the pain of seeing you refuse me help in this extremity! Nevertheless, I am not going to dwell upon the consequences—for I do not wish to owe anything to your pity.

Verdelin (taking a seat)

A thousand crowns! But what purpose would you apply them to?

Mercadet (aside) I shall get them. (Aloud) My dear fellow, a son-in-law is a bird who is easily frightened away. The absence of one piece of lace on a dress reveals everything to them. The ladies' costumes are ordered, the merchants are on the point of delivering them—yes, I was rash enough to say that I would pay for everything, for I counted on you! Verdelin, a thousand crowns won't kill you, for you have sixty thousand francs a year. And the life of a young girl of whom you are fond is now at stake—for you are fond of Julie! She has a sincere attachment for your little girl, they play together like the happiest of creatures. Would you let the companion of your daughter pine away with despair? Misfortune is contagious! It brings evil on all around!

Verdelin My dear fellow, I have not a thousand crowns. I can lend you my plate; but I have not—

Mercadet

You can give me your note on the bank. It is soon signed—

Verdelin (rising)

I—no—

Mercadet Ah! my poor daughter! It is all over. (Falls back overcome in an armchair near the table.) God forgive me, if I put an end to the painful dream of life, and let me awaken in Thy bosom!

Verdelin (after a short silence)

But— Have you really found a son-in-law?

Mercadet (rising abruptly to his feet) You ask if I have found a son-in-law! You actually throw a doubt upon this! You may refuse me, if you like, the means of effecting the happiness of my daughter, but do not insult me! I am fallen low indeed! O Verdelin! I would not for a thousand crowns have had such an idea of you, and you can never win absolution from me excepting by giving them.

Verdelin (wishing to leave)

I must go and see if I can—

Mercadet No! This is only another way of refusing me! Can I believe it? Will not you whom I have seen spend the same sum upon some such trifle as a passing love affair—will you not apply the thousand crowns to the performance of a good action?

Verdelin (laughing)

At the present time there are very few good actions, or transactions.

Mercadet

Ha! Ha! Ha! How witty! You are laughing, I see there is a reaction!

Verdelin

Ha! Ha! Ha! (He drops his hat.)

Mercadet (picking up the hat and dusting it with his sleeve) Come now, old fellow. Haven't we seen life! We two began it together. What a lot of things we have said and done! Don't you recollect the good old time when we swore to be friends always through thick and thin?

Verdelin

Indeed, I do. And don't you recollect our party at Rambouillet, where I fought an officer of the Guard on your account?

Mercadet I thought it was for the lovely Clarissa! Ah! But we were gay! We were young! And to-day we have our daughters, daughters old enough to marry! If Clarissa were alive now, she would blame your hesitation!

Verdelin

If she had lived, I should never have married.

Mercadet Because you know what love is, that you do! So I may count upon you for dinner, and you give me your word of honor that you will send me—

Verdelin

The plate?

Mercadet

And the thousand crowns—

Verdelin

Ah! You still harp upon that! I have told you I cannot do it.

Mercadet (aside) It is certain that this fellow will never die of heart failure. (Aloud) And so it seems I am to be murdered by my best friend? Alas! It is always thus! You are actually untouched by the memory of Clarissa—and by the despair of a father! (He cries out towards the chamber of his wife.) Ah! it is all over! I am in despair! I am going to blow my brains out!

SCENE THIRTEENTH

The same persons, Mme. Mercadet and Julie.

Mme. Mercadet

What on earth is the matter with you, my dear?

Julie

How your voice frightened us, papa!

Mercadet They heard us! See how they come, like two guardian angels! (He takes them by the hand.) Ah! you melt my heart! (To Verdelin) Verdelin! Do you wish to slay a whole family? This proof of their tenderness gives me courage to fall at your feet.

Julie Oh, sir! (She checks her father.) It is I who will implore you for him. Whatever may be his demand, do not refuse my father; he must, indeed, be in the most terrible anguish!

Mercadet Dear child! (Aside) In what accents does she speak! I couldn't speak so naturally as that.

Mme. Mercadet

M. Verdelin, listen to us—

Verdelin (to Julie)

You don't know what he is asking, do you?

Julie

No.

Verdelin

He is asking for a thousand crowns, in order to arrange your marriage.

Julie Then, forget, sir, all that I said to you; I do not wish for a marriage which has been purchased by the humiliation of my father.

Mercadet (aside)

She is magnificent!

Verdelin

Julie! I will go at once and get the money for you. (Exit.)

SCENE FOURTEENTH

The same persons, except Verdelin; then the servants.

Julie

Oh, father! Why did you not tell me?

Mercadet (kissing her) You have saved us all! Ah! when shall I be so rich and powerful that I may make him repent of a favor done so grudgingly?

Mme. Mercadet

Do not be unjust; Verdelin yielded to your request.

Mercadet He yielded to the cry of Julie, not to my request. Ah! my dear, he has extorted from me more than a thousand crowns' worth of humiliation!

Justin (coming in with Therese and Virginie)

The tradespeople.

Virginie

The milliner and the dressmaker—

Therese

And the dry-goods merchants.

Mercadet That is all right! I have succeeded in my scheme! My daughter shall be Comtesse de la Brive! (To the servants) Show them in! I am waiting, and the money is ready. (He goes proudly towards his study, while the servants look at him with surprise.)

Curtain to the First Act.

ACT II

SCENE FIRST

(Mercadet's study, containing book-shelves, a safe, a desk, an armchair and a sofa.)

Minard and Justin, then Julie.

Minard

Did you say that M. Mercadet wished to speak with me?

Justin

Yes, sir. But mademoiselle has requested that you await her here.

Minard (aside) Her father asks to see me. She wishes to speak to me before the interview. Something extraordinary must have happened.

Justin

Mademoiselle is here.

(Enter Julie.)

Minard (going towards her)

Mlle. Julie!

Julie Justin, inform my father that the gentleman has arrived. (Exit Justin.) If you wish, Adolphe, that our love should shine as bright in the sight of all as it does in our hearts, be as courageous as I have already been.

Minard

What has taken place?

Julie A rich young suitor has presented himself, and my father is acting without any pity for us.

Minard

A rival! And you ask me if I have any courage! Tell me his name, Julie, and you will soon know whether I have any courage.

Julie Adolphe! You make me shudder! Is this the way in which you are going to act with the hope of bending my father?

Minard (seeing Mercadet approach)

Here he comes.

SCENE SECOND

The same persons and Mercadet.

Mercadet

Sir, are you in love with my daughter?

Minard

Yes, sir.

Mercadet That is, at least, what she believes, and you seem to have had the talent to persuade her that it is so.

Minard Your manner of expressing yourself implies a doubt on your part, which in any one else would have been offensive to me. Why should I not love mademoiselle? Abandoned by my parents, it was from your daughter, sir, that I have learned for the first time the happiness of affection. Mlle. Julie is at the same time a sister and a friend to me. She is my whole family. She alone has smiled upon me and has encouraged me; and my love for her is beyond what language can express!

Julie

Must I remain here, father?

Mercadet (to his daughter) Swallow it all! (To Minard) Sir, with regard to the love of young people I have those positive ideas which are considered peculiar to old men. My distrust of such love is all the more permissible because I am not the father blinded by paternal affection. I see Julie exactly as she is; without being absolutely plain, she has none of that beauty that makes people cry out, "See!" She is quite mediocre.

Minard You are mistaken, sir; I venture to say that you do not know your daughter.

Mercadet

Permit me—

Minard

You do not know her, sir.

Mercadet

But I know her perfectly well—as if—in a word, I know her—

Minard

No, sir, you do not.

Mercadet

Do you mean to contradict me again, sir?

Minard You know the Julie that all the world sees; but love has transfigured her! Tenderness and devotion lend to her a transporting beauty that I alone have called up in her.

Julie

Father, I feel ashamed—

Mercadet

You mean you feel happy. And if you, sir, repeat these things—

Minard I shall repeat them a hundred times, a thousand times, and even then I couldn't repeat them often enough. There is no crime in repeating them before a father!

Mercadet You flatter me! I did believe myself her father; but you are the father of a Julie whose acquaintance I should very much like to make.

Minard

You have never been in love, I suppose?

Mercadet I have been very much in love! And felt the galling chain of gold like everybody else.

Minard

That was long ago. In these days we love in a better way.

Mercadet

How do you do that?

Minard

We cling to the soul, to the idea!

Mercadet

What we used to call under the Empire, having our eyes bandaged.

Minard It is love, pure and holy, which can lend a charm to all the hours of life.

Mercadet

Yes all!—except the dinner hour.

Julie Father, do not ridicule two children who love each other with a passion which is true and pure, because it is founded upon a knowledge of each other's character; on the certitude of their mutual ardor in conquering the difficulties of life; in a word, of two children who will also cherish sincere affection for you.

Minard (to Mercadet)

What an angel, sir!

Mercadet (aside) I'll angel you! (Putting an arm around each.) Happy children! — You are absolutely in love? What a fine romance! (To Minard) You desire her for your wife?

Minard

Yes, sir.

Mercadet

In spite of all obstacles?

Minard

It is mine to overcome them!

Julie Father, ought you not to be grateful to me in that by my choice I am giving you a son full of lofty sentiments, endowed with a courageous soul, and—

Minard

Mademoiselle—Julie.

Julie

Let me finish; I must have my say.

Mercadet My daughter, go and see your mother, and let me speak of matters which are a great deal more material than these.

Julie

I will go, father—

Mercadet

Come back presently with your mother, my child.

(Mercadet kisses Julie and leads her to the door.)

Minard (aside)

I feel my hopes revive.

Mercadet (returning)

Sir, I am a ruined man.

Minard

What does that mean?

Mercadet Totally ruined. And if you wish to have my Julie, you are welcome to her. She will be much better off at your house, poor as you are, than in her paternal home. Not only is she without dowry, but she is burdened with poor parents—parents who are more than poor.

Minard

More than poor! There is nothing beyond that.

Mercadet Yes, sir, we are in debt, deeply in debt, and some of these debts clamor for payment.

Minard

No, no, it is impossible!

Mercadet Don't you believe it? (Aside) He is getting frightened. (Taking up a pile of papers from his desk. Aloud) Here, my would-be son-in-law, are the family papers which will show you our fortune—

Minard

Sir—

Mercadet Or rather our lack of fortune! Read— Here is a writ of attachment on our furniture.

Minard

Can it be possible?

Mercadet It is perfectly possible! Here are judgments by the score! Here is a writ of my arrest. You see in what straits we are! Here you see all my sales, the protests on my notes and the judgments classed in order— for, young man, understand well in a disordered condition of things, order is above all things necessary. When disorder is well arranged it can be relieved and controlled— What can a debtor say when he sees his debt entered up under his number? I make the government my model. All payments are made in alphabetic order. I have not yet touched the letter A. (He replaces the papers.)

Minard

You haven't yet paid anything?

Mercadet Scarcely anything. You know the condition of my expenses. You know, because you are a book-keeper. See, (picking up the papers again) the total debit is three hundred and eighty thousand.

Minard

Yes, sir. The balance is entered here.

Mercadet You can understand then how you must make me shudder when you come before my daughter with your fine protestations! Since to marry a poor girl with nothing but an income of eighteen hundred francs, is like inviting in wedlock a protested note with a writ of execution.

Minard (lost in thought)

Ruined, ruined! And without resources!

Mercadet (aside) I thought that would upset him. (Aloud) Come, now, young man, what are you going to do?

Minard

First, I thank you, sir, for the frankness of your admissions.

Mercadet

That is good! And what of the ideal, and your love for my daughter?

Minard

You have opened my eyes, sir.

Mercadet (aside)

I am glad to hear it.

Minard I thought that I already loved her with a love that was boundless, and now I love her a hundred times more.

Mercadet

The deuce you do!

Minard Have you not led me to understand that she will have need of all my courage, of all my devotion! I will render her happy by other means than my tenderness; she shall feel grateful for all my efforts, she shall love me for my vigils, and for my toils.

Mercadet

You mean to tell me that you still wish to marry her?

Minard Do I wish! When I believed that you were rich, I would not ask her of you without trembling, without feeling ashamed of my poverty; but now, sir, it is with assurance and with tranquillity of mind that I ask for her.

Mercadet (to himself)

I must admit that this is a love exceedingly true, sincere and noble!

And such as I had believed it impossible to find in the whole world! (To Minard) Forgive me, young man, for the opinion I had of you—forgive me, above all, for the disappointment I am about to cause you.

Minard

What do you mean?

Mercadet

M. Minard—Julie—cannot be your wife.

Minard What is this, sir? Not be my wife? In spite of our love, in spite of all you have confided to me?

Mercadet Yes, and just because of all I have confided to you. I have shown you Mercadet the rich man in his true colors. I am going to show you him as the skeptical man of business. I have frankly opened my books to you. I am now going to open my heart to you as frankly.

Minard

Speak out, sir, but remember how great my devotion to Mlle. Julie is. Remember that my self-sacrifice and unselfishness are equal to my love for her.

Mercadet Let it be granted that by means of night-long vigils and toils you will make a living for Julie! But who will make a living for us, her father and mother?

Minard

Ah! sir—believe in me!

Mercadet

What! Are you going to work for four, instead of working for only two? The task will be too much for you! And the bread which you give to us, you will have to snatch out of the hands of your children—

Minard

How wildly you talk!

Mercadet And I, in spite of your generous efforts, shall fall, crushed under the weight of disgraceful ruin. A brilliant marriage for my daughter is the only means by which I would be enabled to discharge the enormous sums I owe. It is only thus that in time I could regain confidence and credit. With the aid of a rich son-in-law I can reconquer my position, and recuperate my fortune! Why, the marriage of my daughter is our last anchor of salvation! This marriage is our hope, our wealth, the prop of our honor, sir! And since you love my daughter, it is to this very love that I make my appeal. My friend, do not condemn her to poverty; do not condemn her to a life of regret over the loss and disgrace which she has brought upon her father!

Minard (in great distress)

But what do you ask me to do?

Mercadet (taking him by the hand) I wish that this noble affection which you have for her, may arm you with more courage than I myself possess.

Minard

I will show such courage —

Mercadet

Then listen to me. If I refuse Julie to you, Julie will refuse the man I destine for her. It will be best, therefore, that I grant your request for her hand, and that you be the one —

Minard

I! — She will not believe it, sir —

Mercadet

She will believe you, if you tell her that you fear poverty for her.

Minard

She will accuse me of being a fortune hunter.

Mercadet

She will be indebted to you for having secured her happiness.

Minard (despairingly)

She will despise me, sir!

Mercadet That is probable! But if I have read your heart aright, your love for her is such that you will sacrifice yourself completely to the happiness of her life. But here she comes, sir, and her mother is with her. It is on their account that I make this request to you, sir; can I count on you?

Minard

You — can.

Mercadet

Very good — I thank you.

SCENE THIRD

The preceding, Julie and Mme. Mercadet.

Julie

Come, mother, I am sure that Adolphe has triumphed over all obstacles.

Mme. Mercadet My dear, M. Minard has asked of you the hand of Julie. What answer have you given him?

Mercadet (going to the desk)

It is for him to say.

Mercadet (aside)

How can I tell her? My heart is breaking.

Julie

What have you got to say, Adolphe?

Minard

Mademoiselle—

Julie Mademoiselle! Am I no longer Julie to you? Oh, tell me quickly. You have settled everything with my father, have you not?

Minard Your father has shown great confidence in me. He has revealed to me his situation; he has told me—

Julie

Go on, please go on—

Mercadet

I have told him that we are ruined—

Julie

And this avowal has not changed your plans—your love—has it,

Adolphe?

Minard (ardently) My love! (Mercadet, without being noticed, seizes his hand.) I should be deceiving you—mademoiselle—(speaking with great effort)—if I were to say that my intentions are unaltered.

Julie

Oh! It is impossible! Can it be you who speak to me in this strain?

Mme. Mercadet

Julie—

Minard (rousing himself) There are some men to whom poverty adds energy; men capable of daily self-sacrifice, of hourly toil; men who think themselves sufficiently recompensed by a smile from a companion that they love—(checking himself). I, mademoiselle am not one of these. The thought of poverty dismays me. I—I could not endure the sight of your unhappiness.

Julie (bursting into tears and flinging herself into the arms of her mother)

Oh! Mother! Mother! Mother!

Mme. Mercadet

My daughter—my poor Julie!

Minard (in a low voice to Mercadet)

Is this sufficient, sir?

Julie (without looking at Minard) I should have had courage for both of us. I should always have greeted you with a smile, I should have toiled without regret, and happiness would always have reigned in our home. You could never have meant this, Adolphe. You do not mean it.

Minard (in a low voice)

Let me go—let me leave the house, sir.

Mercadet

Come, then. (He retires to the back of the stage.)

Minard Good-bye—Julie. A love that would have flung you into poverty is a thoughtless love. I have preferred to show the love that sacrifices itself to your happiness—

Julie No, I trust you no longer. (In a low voice to her mother) My only happiness would have been to be his.

Justin (announcing visitors)

M. de la Brive! M. de Mericourt!

Mercadet Take your daughter away, madame. M. Minard, follow me. (To Justin) Ask them to wait here for a while. (To Minard) I am well satisfied with you.

(Mme. Mercadet and Julie, Mercadet and Minard go out in opposite directions, while Justin admits Mericourt and De la Brive.)

SCENE FOURTH

De la Brive and Mericourt.

Justin

M. Mercadet begs that the gentlemen will wait for him here. (Exit.)

Mericourt At last, my dear friend, you are on the ground, and you will be very soon officially recognized as Mlle. Mercadet's intended! Steer your bark well, for the father is a deep one.

De la Brive

That is what frightens me, for difficulties loom ahead.

Mericourt I do not believe so; Mercadet is a speculator, rich to-day, to-morrow possibly a beggar. With the little I know of his affairs from his wife, I am led to believe that he is enchanted with the prospect of depositing a part of his fortune in the name of his daughter, and of obtaining a son-in-law capable of assisting him in carrying out his financial schemes.

De la Brive That is a good idea, and suits me exactly; but suppose he wishes to find out too much about me.

Mericourt

I have given M. Mercadet an excellent account of you.

De la Brive

I have fallen upon my feet truly.

Mericourt But you are not going to lose the dandy's self-possession? I quite understand that your position is risky. A man would not marry, excepting from utter despair. Marriage is suicide for the man of the world. (In a low voice) Come, tell me—can you hold out much longer?

De la Brive If I had not two names, one for the bailiffs and one for the fashionable world, I should be banished from the Boulevard. Woman and I, as you know, have wrought each the ruin of the other, and, as fashion now goes, to find a rich Englishwoman, an amiable dowager, an amorous gold mine, would be as impossible as to find an extinct animal.

Mericourt

What of the gaming table?

De la Brive Oh! Gambling is an unreliable resource excepting for certain crooks, and I am not such a fool as to run the risk of disgrace for the sake of winnings which always have their limit. Publicity, my dear friend, has been the abolition of all those shady careers in which fortune once was to be found. So, that for a hundred thousand francs of accepted bills, the usurer gives me but ten thousand. Pierquin sent me to one of his agents, a sort of sub-Pierquin, a little old man called Violette, who said to my broker that he could not give me money on such paper at any rate! Meanwhile my tailor has refused to bank upon my prospects. My horse is living on credit; as to my tiger, the little wretch who wears such fine clothes, I do now know how he lives, or where he feeds. I dare not peer into the mystery. Now, as we are not so advanced in civilization as the Jews, who canceled all debts every half-century, a man must pay by the sacrifice of personal liberty. Horrible things will be said about me. Here is a young man of high esteem in the world of fashion, pretty lucky at cards, of a passable figure, less than twenty-eight years old, and he is going to marry the daughter of a rich speculator!

Mericourt

What difference does it make?

De la Brive It is slightly off color! But I am tired of a sham life. I have learned at last that the only way to amass wealth is to work. But our misfortune is that we find ourselves quick at everything, but not good at anything! A man like me, capable of inspiring a passion and of maintaining it, cannot become either a clerk or a soldier! Society has provided no employment for us. Accordingly, I am going to set up business with Mercadet. He is one of the greatest of schemers. You are sure that he won't give less than a hundred and fifty thousand francs to his daughter.

Mericourt Judge yourself, my dear friend, from the style which Mme. Mercadet puts on; you see her at all the first nights, in her own box, at the opera, and her conspicuous elegance—

De la Brive

I myself am elegant enough, but—

Mericourt Look round you here—everything indicates opulence—Oh! they are well off!

De la Brive Yet, it is a sort of middle-class splendor, something substantial which promises well.

Mericourt And then the mother is a woman of principle, of irreproachable behavior. Can you possibly conclude matters to-day?

De la Brive I have taken steps to do so. I won at the club yesterday sufficient to go on with; I shall pay something on the wedding presents, and let the balance stand.

Mericourt

Without reckoning my account, what is the amount of your debts?

De la Brive A mere trifle! A hundred and fifty thousand francs, which my father-in-law will cut down to fifty thousand. I shall have a hundred thousand francs left to begin life on. I always said that I should never become rich until I hadn't a sou left.

Mericourt Mercadet is an astute man; he will question you about your fortune; are you prepared?

De la Brive Am I not the landed proprietor of La Brive? Three thousand acres in the Landes, which are worth thirty thousand francs, mortgaged for forty-five thousand and capable of being floated by a stock jobbing company for some commercial purpose or other, say, as representing a capital of a hundred thousand crowns! You cannot imagine how much this property has brought me in.

Mericourt Your name, your horse, and your lands seem to me to be on their last legs.

De la Brive

Not so loud!

Mericourt

So you have quite made up your mind?

De la Brive

Yes, and all the more decidedly in that I am going into politics.

Mericourt

Really—but you are too clever for that!

De la Brive

As a preparation I shall take to journalism.

Mericourt

And you have never written two lines in your life!

De la Brive There are journalists who write and journalists who do not write. The former are editors—and horses that drag the car; the latter, the proprietors, who furnish the funds; these give oats to their horses and keep the capital for themselves. I shall be a proprietor. You merely have to put on a lofty air and exclaim: "The Eastern question is a question of great importance and of wide influence, one about which there cannot be two opinions!" You sum up a discussion by declaiming: "England, sir, will always get the better of us!" or you make an answer to some one whom you have heard speak for a long time without paying attention to him: "We are advancing towards an abyss, we have not yet passed through all the evolutions of the evolutionary phase!" You say to a representative of labor: "Sir, I think there is something to be done in this matter." A proprietor of a journal speaks very little, rushes about and makes himself useful by doing for a man in power what the latter cannot do himself. He is supposed to inspire the articles, those I mean, which attract any notice! And then, if it is absolutely necessary he undertakes to publish a yellow-backed volume on some Utopian topic, so well written, so strong, that no one opens it, although every one declares that he has read it! Then he is looked upon as an earnest man, and ends by finding himself acknowledged as somebody, instead of something.

Mericourt

Alas! What you say is too true, in these times!

De la Brive And we ourselves are a startling proof of this! In order to claim a part in political power you must not show what good but what harm you can do. You must not alone possess talents, you must be able also to inspire fear. Accordingly, the very day after my marriage, I shall assume an air of seriousness, of profundity, of high principles! I can take my choice, for we have in France a list of principles which is as varied as a bill of fare. I elect to be a socialist! The word pleases me! At every epoch, my dear friend, there are adjectives which form the pass-words of ambition! Before 1789 a man called himself an economist; in 1815 he was a liberal; the next party will call itself the social party—perhaps because it is so unsocial. For in France you must always take the opposite sense of a word to understand its meaning.

Mericourt Let me tell you privately, that you are now talking nothing but the nonsense of masked ball chatter, which passes for wit among those who do not indulge in it. What are you going to do when a certain definite knowledge becomes necessary?

De la Brive My dear friend! In every profession, whether of art, science or literature, a man needs intellectual capital, special knowledge and capacity. But in politics, my dear fellow, a man wins everything and attains to everything by means of a single phrase—

Mericourt

What is that?

De la Brive "The principles of my friends, the party for which I stand, look for—"

Mericourt

Hush! Here comes the father-in-law!

SCENE FIFTH

The same persons and Mercadet.

Mercadet Good-day, my dear Mericourt! (To De la Brive) The ladies have kept you waiting, sir. Ah! They are putting on their finery. For myself, I was just on the point of dismissing—whom do you think?—an aspirant to the hand of Mlle. Julie. Poor young man! I was perhaps hard on him, and yet I felt for him. He worships my daughter; but what could I do? He has only ten thousand francs' income.

De la Brive

That wouldn't go very far!

Mercadet

A mere subsistence!

De la Brive

You're not the man to give a rich and clever girl to the first comer—

Mericourt

Certainly not.

Mercadet Before the ladies come in, gentlemen, we must talk a little serious business.

De la Brive (to Mericourt)

Now comes the tug of war!

(They all sit down.)

Mercadet (on the sofa)

Are you seriously in love with my daughter?

De la Brive

I love her passionately!

Mercadet

Passionately?

Mericourt (to his friend)

You are over-doing it.

De la Brive (to Mericourt) Wait a moment. (Aloud) Sir, I am ambitious—and I saw in Mlle. Julie a lady at once distinguished, full of intellect, possessed of charming manners, who would never be out of place in the position in which my fortune puts me; and such a wife is essential to the success of a politician.

Mercadet I understand! It is easy to find a woman, but it is very rare that a man who wishes to be a minister or ambassador finds a wife. You are a man of wit, sir. May I ask your political leaning?

De la Brive

Sir, I am a socialist.

Mercadet

That is a new move! But now let us talk of money matters.

Mericourt

It seems to me that the notary might attend to that.

De la Brive No! M. Mercadet is right; it is best that we should attend to these things ourselves.

Mercadet

True, sir.

De la Brive Sir, my whole fortune consists in the estate which bears my name; it has been in my family for a hundred and fifty years, and I hope will never pass from us.

Mercadet The possession of capital is perhaps more valuable in these days. Capital is in your own hand. If a revolution breaks out, and we have had many revolutions lately, capital follows us everywhere. Landed property, on the contrary, must furnish funds for every one. There it stands stock still like a fool to pay the taxes, while capital dodges out of the way. But this is not real obstacle. What is the amount of your land?

De la Brive

Three thousand acres, without a break.

Mercadet

Without a break?

Mericourt

Did I not tell you as much?

Mercadet

I never doubted it.

De la Brive

A chateau—

Mercadet

Good—

De la Brive And salt marshes, which can be worked as soon as the administration gives permission. They would yield enormous returns!

Mercadet Ah, sir, why have we been so late in becoming acquainted! Your land, then, must be on the seashore.

De la Brive

Without half a league of it.

Mercadet

And it is situated?

De la Brive

Near Bordeaux.

Mercadet

You have vineyards, then?

De la Brive No! fortunately not, for the disposal of wines is a troublesome matter, and, moreover, the cultivation of the vine is exceedingly expensive. My estate was planted with pine trees by my grandfather, a man of genius, who was wise enough to sacrifice himself to the welfare of his descendants. Besides, I have furniture, which you know—

Mercadet

Sir, one moment, a man of business is always careful to dot his i's.

De la Brive (under his voice)

Now we're in for it!

Mercadet With regard to your estate and your marshes,—I see all that can be got out of these marshes. The best way of utilizing them would be to form a company for the exploitation of the marshes of the Brive! There is more than a million in it!

De la Brive I quite understand that, sir. They need only to be thrown upon the market.

Mercadet (aside)

These words indicate a certain intelligence in this young man. (Aloud) Have you any debts? Is your estate mortgaged?

Mericourt

You would not think much of my friend if he had not debts.

De la Brive I will be frank, sir, there is a mortgage of forty-five thousand francs on my estate.

Mercadet (aside)

An innocent young man! he might easily— (Rising from his seat. Aloud) You have my consent; you shall be my son-in-law, and are the very man I would choose for my daughter's husband. You do not realize what a fortune you possess.

De la Brive (to Mericourt)

This is almost too good to be true.

Mericourt (to De la Brive)

He is dazzled by the good speculation which he sees ahead.

Mercadet (aside) With government protection, which can be purchased, salt pits may be established. I am saved! (Aloud) Allow me to shake hands with you, after the English fashion. You fulfill all that I expected in a son-in-law. I plainly see you have none of the narrowness of provincial landholders; we shall understand each other thoroughly. De la Brive

You must not take it in bad part, sir, if I, on my part, ask you—

Mercadet The amount of my daughter's fortune? I should have distrusted you if you hadn't asked! My daughter has independent means; her mother settles on her her own fortune, consisting of a small property—a farm of two hundred acres, but in the very heart of Brie, and provided with good buildings. Besides this, I shall give her two hundred thousand francs, the interest of which will be for your use, until you find a suitable investment for it. So you see, young man, we do not wish to deceive you, we wish to keep the money moving; I like you, you please me, for I see you have ambition.

De la Brive

Yes, sir.

Mercadet

You love luxury, extravagance; you wish to shine at Paris—

De la Brive

Yes, sir.

Mercadet You see that I am already an old man, obliged to lay the load of my ambition upon some congenial co-operator, and you shall be the one to play the brilliant part.

De la Brive

Sir, had I been obliged to take my choice of all the fathers-in-law in Paris, I should have given the preference to you. You are a man after my own heart! Allow me to shake hands, after the English fashion!

(They shake hands for the second time.)

Mercadet (aside)

It seems too good to be true.

De la Brive (aside)

He fell head-first into my salt marshes!

Mercadet (aside)

He accepts an income from me!

(Mercadet retires towards the door on the left side.)

Mericourt (to De la Brive)

Are you satisfied?

De la Brive (to Mericourt)

I don't see the money for my debts.

Mericourt (to De la Brive) Wait a moment. (To Mercadet) My friend does not dare to tell you of it, but he is too honest for concealment. He has a few debts.

Mercadet Oh, please tell me. I understand perfectly—I suppose it is about fifty thousand you owe?

Mericourt

Very nearly—

De la Brive

Very nearly—

Mercadet

A mere trifle.

De la Brive (laughing)

Yes, a mere trifle!

Mercadet They will serve as a subject of discussion between your wife and you; yes, let her have the pleasure of— But, we will pay them all. (Aside) In shares of the La Brive salt pits. (Aloud) It is so small an amount. (Aside) We will put up the capital of the salt marsh a hundred thousand francs more. (Aloud) The matter is settled, son-in-law.

De la Brive

We will consider it settled, father-in-law.

Mercadet (aside)

I am saved!

De la Brive (aside)

I am saved!

SCENE SIXTH

The same persons, Mme. Mercadet and Julie.

Mercadet

Here are my wife and daughter.

Mericourt Madame, allow me to present to you my friend, M. de la Brive, who regards your daughter with—

De la Brive

With passionate admiration.

Mercadet

My daughter is exactly the woman to suit a politician.

De la Brive (to Mericourt. Gazing at Julie through his eyeglass)

A fine girl. (To Madame Mercadet) Like mother, like daughter. Madame, I place my hopes under your protection.

Mme. Mercadet

Anyone introduced by M. Mericourt would be welcome here.

Julie (to her father)

What a coxcomb!

Mercadet (to his daughter) He is enormously rich. We shall all be millionaires! He is an excessively clever fellow. Now, do try and be amiable, as you ought to be.

Julie (answering him) What would you wish me to say to a dandy whom I have just seen for the first time, and whom you destine for my husband?

De la Brive May I be permitted to hope, mademoiselle, that you will look favorably upon me?

Julie

My duty is to obey my father.

De la Brive

Young people are not always aware of the feelings which they inspire.

For two months I have been longing for the happiness of paying my respects to you.

Julie Who can be more flattered than I am, sir, to find that I have attracted your attention?

Mme. Mercadet (to Mericourt)

He is a fine fellow. (Aloud) We hope that you and your friend M. de la Brive will do us the pleasure of accepting our invitation to dine without ceremony?

Mercadet To take pot-luck with us. (To De la Brive) You must excuse our simplicity.

Justin (entering, in a low voice to Mercadet)

M. Pierquin wishes to speak to you, monsieur.

Mercadet (low)

Pierquin?

Justin

He says it is concerning an important and urgent matter.

Mercadet What can he want with me? Let him come in. (Justin goes out. Aloud) My dear, these gentlemen must be tired. Won't you take them into the drawing-room? M. de la Brive, give my daughter you arm.

De la Brive

Mademoiselle— (offers her his arm)

Julie (aside)

He is handsome, he is rich—why does he choose me?

Mme. Mercadet M. de Mericourt, will you come and see the picture which we are going to raffle off for the benefit of the poor orphans?

Mericourt

With pleasure, madame.

Mercadet

Go on. I shall be with you in a moment.

SCENE SEVENTH

Mercadet (alone) Well, after all, this time I have really secured fortune and the happiness of Julie and the rest of us. For a son-in-law like this is a veritable gold mine! Three thousand acres! A chateau! Salt marshes! (He sits down at his desk.)

Pierquin (entering)

Good-day, Mercadet. I have come—

Mercadet

Rather inopportunely. But what do you wish?

Pierquin I sha'n't detain you long. The bills of exchange I gave you this morning, signed by a man called Michonnin, are absolutely valueless. I told you this beforehand.

Mercadet

I know that.

Pierquin

I now offer you a thousand crowns for them.

Mercadet That is either too much or too little! Anything for which you will give that sum must be worth infinitely more. Some one is waiting for me in the other room. I will bid you good-evening.

Pierquin

I will give you four thousand francs.

Mercadet

No!

Pierquin

Five—six thousand.

Mercadet If you wish to play cards, keep to the gambling table. Why do you wish to recover this paper?

Pierquin Michonnin has insulted me. I wish to take vengeance on him; to send him to jail.

Mercadet (rising) Six thousand francs worth of vengeance! You are not a man to indulge in luxuries of that kind.

Pierquin

I assure you—

Mercadet Come, now, my friend, consider that for a satisfactory defamation of character the code won't charge you more than five or six hundred francs, and the tax on a blow is only fifty francs—

Pierquin

I swear to you—

Mercadet Has this Michonnin come into a legacy? And are the forty-seven thousand francs of these vouchers actually worth forty-seven thousand francs? You should post me on this subject and then we'll cry halves!

Pierquin

Very well, I agree. The fact of it is, Michonnin is to be married.

Mercadet

What next! And with whom, pray?

Pierquin With the daughter of some nabob—an idiot who is giving her an enormous dowry.

Mercadet

Where does Michonnin live?

Pierquin Do you want to issue a writ? He is without a fixed abode in Paris. His furniture is held under the name of a friend; but his legal domicile must be in the neighborhood of Bordeaux, in the village of Ermont.

Mercadet Stay a while. I have some one here from that region. I can get exact information in a moment—and then we can begin proceedings.

Pierquin

Send me the paper, and leave the business to me—

Mercadet I shall be very glad to do so. They shall be put into your hands in return for a signed agreement as to the sharing of the money. I am at present altogether taken up with the marriage of my daughter.

Pierquin

I hope everything is going on well.

Mercadet Wonderfully well. My son-in-law is a gentleman and, in spite of that, he is rich. And, although both rich and a gentleman, he is clever into the bargain.

Pierquin

I congratulate you.

Mercadet One word with you before you go. You said, Michonnin, of Ermont, in the neighborhood of Bordeaux?

Pierquin Yes, he has an old aunt somewhere about there! A good woman called Bourdillac, who scrapes along on some six hundred francs a year, but to whom he gives the title of Marchioness of Bourdillac. He pretends that her health is delicate and that she has a yearly income of forty thousand francs.

Mercadet

Thank you. Good-evening—

Pierquin

Good-evening. (goes out)

Mercadet (ringing)

Justin!

Justin

Did you call, sir?

Mercadet

Ask M. de la Brive to speak with me for a moment. (Justin goes out.)

Mercadet Here is a windfall of twenty-three thousand francs! We shall be able to arrange things famously for Julie's marriage.

SCENE EIGHTH

Mercadet, De la Brive and Justin.

De la Brive (to Justin, handing him a letter)

Here, deliver this letter. And this is for yourself.

Justin (aside)

A louis! Mademoiselle will be sure to have a happy home. (Exit.)

De la Brive

You wish to speak with me, my dear father-in-law?

Mercadet Yes. You see I already treat you without ceremony. Please to take a seat.

De la Brive (sitting on a sofa)

I am grateful for your confidence.

Mercadet I am seeking information with regard to a debtor, who, like you, lives in the neighborhood of Bordeaux.

De la Brive

I know every one in that district.

Mercadet

It is said he has relations there.

De la Brive

Relations! I have none but an old aunt.

Mercadet (pricking up his ears)

An—old aunt—?

De la Brive

Whose health—

Mercadet (trembling)

Is—is—delicate?

De la Brive

And her income is forty thousand francs.

Mercadet (quite overcome)

Good Lord! The very figure!

De la Brive The Marchioness, you see, will be a good woman to have on hand. I mean the Marchioness—

Mercadet (vehemently rushing at him)

Of Bourdillac, sir!

De la Brive

How is this? Do you know her name?

Mercadet

Yes, and yours too!

De la Brive

The devil you do!

Mercadet You are head over ears in debt; your furniture is held in another man's name; your old aunt has a pittance of six hundred francs; Pierquin, who is one of your smallest creditors, has forty-seven thousand francs in notes of hand from you. You are Michonnin, and I am the idiotic nabob!

De la Brive (stretching himself at full length on the sofa)

By heavens! You know just as much about it as I do!

Mercadet

Well—I see that once more the devil has taken a hand in my game.

De la Brive (aside, rising to his feet) The marriage is over! I am no longer a socialist; I shall become a communist.

Mercadet

And I have been just as easily deceived, as if I had been on the

Exchange.

De la Brive

Show yourself worthy of your reputation.

Mercadet

M. Michonnin, your conduct is more than blameworthy!

De la Brive

In what particular? Did I not say that I had debts?

Mercadet We'll let that pass, for any one may have debts; but where is your estate situated.

De la Brive

In the Landes.

Mercadet

And of what does it consist?

De la Brive

Of sand wastes, planted with firs.

Mercadet

Good to make toothpicks.

De la Brive

That's about it.

Mercadet

And it is worth?

De la Brive

Thirty thousand francs.

Mercadet

And mortgaged for—

De la Brive

Forty-five thousand!

Mercadet

And you had the skill to effect that?

De la Brive

Why, yes—

Mercadet

Damnation! But that was pretty clever! And your marshes, sir?

De la Brive

They border on the sea—

Mercadet

They are part of the ocean!

De la Brive The people of that country are evil-minded enough to say so. That is what hinders my loans!

Mercadet It would be very difficult to issue ocean shares! Sir, I may tell you, between ourselves, that your morality seems to me—

De la Brive

Somewhat—

Mercadet

Risky.

De la Brive (in anger)

Sir! (calming himself) Let this be merely between ourselves!

Mercadet

You gave a friend a bill of sale of your furniture, you sign your

notes of hand with the name of Michonnin, and you call yourself merely

De la Brive—

De la Brive

Well, sir, what are you going to do about it?

Mercadet

Do about it? I am going to lead you a pretty dance—

De la Brive Sir, I am your guest! Moreover, I may deny everything— What proofs have you?

Mercadet What proofs! I have in my hands forty-seven thousand francs' worth of your notes.

De la Brive

Are they signed to the order of Pierquin?

Mercadet

Precisely so.

De la Brive

And you have had them since this morning?

Mercadet

Since this morning.

De la Brive

I see. You have given worthless stock in exchange for valueless notes.

Mercadet

Sir!

De la Brive And, in order to seal the bargain, Pierquin, one of the least important of your creditors, has given you a delay of three months.

Mercadet

Who told you that?

De la Brive Who? Who? Pierquin himself, of course, as soon as he learned I was going to make an arrangement—

Mercadet

The devil he did!

De la Brive Ah! You were going to give two hundred thousand francs as a dowry to your daughter, and you had debts to the amount of three hundred and fifty thousand! Between ourselves it looks like you who had been trying to swindle the son-in-law, sir—

Mercadet (angrily)

Sir! (calming himself) This is merely between ourselves, sir.

De la Brive

You took advantage of my inexperience!

Mercadet Of course I did! The inexperience of a man who raises a loan on his sand wastes fifty per cent above their value.

De la Brive

Glass can be made out of sand!

Mercadet

That's a good idea!

De la Brive

Therefore, sir—

Mercadet Silence! Promise me that this broken marriage-contract shall be kept secret.

De la Brive I swear it shall— Ah! excepting to Pierquin. I have just written to him to set his mind at rest.

Mercadet

Is that the letter you sent by Justin?

De la Brive

The very one.

Mercadet

And what have you told him?

De la Brive

The name of my father-in-law. Confound it!—I thought you were rich.

Mercadet (despairingly) And you have written that to Pierquin? It's all up! This fresh defeat will be known on the Exchange! But, any way, I am ruined! Suppose I write to him— Suppose I ask him— (He goes to the table to write.)

SCENE NINTH

The same persons, Mme. Mercadet, Julie and Verdelin.

Mme. Mercadet

My friend, M. Verdelin.

Julie (to Verdelin)

Here is my father, sir.

Mercadet

Ah! It is you, is it, Verdelin—and you are come to dinner?

Verdelin

No, I am not come to dinner.

Mercadet (aside)

He knows all. He is furious!

Verdelin

And this gentleman is your son-in-law? (Verdelin bows to De la Brive.) This is a fine marriage you are going to make!

Mercadet

The marriage, my dear sir, is not going to take place.

Julie

How happy I feel!

(De la Brive bows to Julie. She casts down her eyes.)

Mme. Mercadet (seizing her hand)

My dear daughter!

Mercadet

I have been deceived by Mericourt.

Verdelin And you have played on me one of your tricks this morning, for the purpose of getting a thousand crowns; but the whole incident has been made public on the Exchange, and they think it a huge joke!

Mercadet

They have been informed, I suppose—

Verdelin That your pocket-book is full of the notes of hand signed by your son-in-law. And Pierquin tells me that your creditors are exasperated, and are to meet to-night at the house of Goulard to conclude measures for united action against you to-morrow!

Mercadet

To-night! To-morrow! Ah! I hear the knell of bankruptcy sound!

Verdelin

Yes, to-morrow they are going to send a prison cab for you.

Mme. Mercadet and Julie

God help us!

Mercadet

I see the carriage, the hearse of the speculator, carrying me to

Clichy!

Verdelin

They wish, as far as possible, to rid the Exchange of all sharpers!

Mercadet They are fools, for in that case they will turn it into a desert! And so I am ruined! Expelled from the Exchange with all the sequelae of bankruptcy,—shame, beggary! I cannot believe it—it is impossible!

De la Brive

Believe me, sir, that I regret having been in some degree—

Mercadet (looking him in the face) You! (in a low voice to him) Listen to me: you have hurried on my destruction, but you have it in your power to help me to escape.

De la Brive

On what conditions?

Mercadet I will make you a good offer! (Aloud, as they start toward opposite doors) True, the idea is a bold one! But to-morrow, the 'Change will recognize in me one of its master spirits.

Verdelin

What is he talking about?

Mercadet To-morrow, all my debts will be paid, and the house of Mercadet will be turning over millions! I shall be acknowledged as the Napoleon of finance.

Verdelin

What a man he is!

Mercadet

And a Napoleon who meets no Waterloo!

Verdelin

But where are your troops?

Mercadet My army is cash in hand! What answer can be made to a business man who says, "Take your money!" Come let us dine now.

Verdelin

Certainly. I shall be delighted to dine with you.

Mercadet (while they all move towards the dining-room, aside) They are all glad of it! To-morrow I will either command millions, or rest in the damp winding-sheet of the Seine!

Curtain to the Second Act.

ACT III

SCENE FIRST

(Another apartment in Mercadet's house, well furnished. At the back and in the centre is a mantel-piece, having instead of a mirror a clear plate of glass; side doors; a large table, surrounded by chairs, in the middle of the stage; sofa and armchairs.)

Justin, Therese and Virginie, then Mercadet.

(Justin enters first and beckons to Therese. Virginie, carrying papers, sits insolently on the sofa. Justin looks through the keyhole of the door on the left side and listens.)

Therese Is it possible that they could pretend to conceal from us the condition of their affairs?

Virginie Old Gruneau tells me that the master is soon to be arrested; I hope that what I have spent will be taken account of, for he owes me the money for these bills, besides my wages!

Therese Oh! set your mind at rest. We are likely to lose everything, for the master is bankrupt.

Justin

I can't hear anything. They speak too low! They don't trust us.

Virginie

It is frightful!

Justin (with his ear to the half-open door)

Wait, I think I hear something.

(The door bursts open and Mercadet appears.)

Mercadet (to Justin)

Don't let me disturb you.

Justin

Sir, I—I—was just putting—

Mercadet Really! (To Virginie, who jumps up suddenly from the sofa) Keep your seat, Mlle. Virginie, and you, M. Justin, why didn't you come in? We were talking about my business.

Justin

You amuse me, sir.

Mercadet

I am heartily glad of it.

Justin

You take trouble easy, sir.

Mercadet (severely) That will do, all of you. And remember that from this time forth I see all who call. Treat no one either with insolence or too much humility, for you will meet here no creditors, but such as have been paid.

Justin

Oh, bosh!

Mercadet

Go!

(The central door opens. Mme. Mercadet, Julie and Minard appear. The servants leave the room.)

SCENE SECOND

Mercadet, Mme. Mercadet, Julie and Minard.

Mercadet (aside) I am annoyed to see my wife and daughter here. In my present circumstances, women are likely to spoil everything, for they have nerves. (Aloud) What is it, Mme. Mercadet?

Mme. Mercadet Sir, you were counting on the marriage of Julie to establish your credit and reassure your creditors, but the event of yesterday has put you at their mercy—

Mercadet

Do you think so? Well, you are quite mistaken. I beg your pardon, M. Minard, but what brings you here?

Minard

Sir—I—

Julie

Father—it is—

Mercadet

Are you come to ask again for my daughter?

Minard

Yes, sir.

Mercadet

But everybody says that I am going to fail—

Minard

I know it, sir.

Mercadet

And would you marry the daughter of a bankrupt?

Minard

Yes, for I would work to re-establish him.

Julie

That's good, Adolphe.

Mercadet (aside) A fine young fellow. I will give him an interest in the first big business I do.

Minard I have made known my attachment to the man I look upon as a father. He has informed me—that I am the possessor of a small fortune—

Mercadet

A fortune!

Minard When I was confided to his care, a sum of money was entrusted to him, which has increased by interest, and I now possess thirty thousand francs.

Mercadet

Thirty thousand francs!

Minard On learning of the disaster that had befallen you, I realized this sum, and I bring it to you, sir; for sometimes in these cases an arrangement can be made by paying something on account—

Mme. Mercadet

He has an excellent heart!

Julie (with pride)

Yes, indeed, papa!

Mercadet Thirty thousand francs. (Aside) They might be tripled by buying some of Verdelin's stock and then doubled with— No, no. (To Minard) My boy, you are at the age of self-sacrifice. If I could pay two hundred francs with thirty thousand, the fortune of France, of myself and of most people would be made. No, keep your money!

Minard

What! You refuse it?

Mercadet (aside) If with this I could keep them quiet for a month, if by some bold stoke I could revive the depression in my property, it might be all right. But the money of these poor children, it cuts me to the heart to think of it, for when they are in tears people calculate amiss; it is not well to risk the money of any but fellow-brokers—no—no (Aloud) Adolphe, you may marry my daughter.

Minard

Oh! Sir—Julie—my own Julie—

Mercadet That is, of course, as soon as she has three hundred thousand francs as dowry.

Mme. Mercadet

My dear!

Julie

Papa!

Minard

Ah, sir! How long are you going to put me off?

Mercadet

Put you off? She will have it in a month! Perhaps sooner—

All

How is that?

Mercadet Yes, by the use of my brains—and a little money. (Minard holds out his pocket-book.) But lock up those bills! And come, take away my wife and daughter. I want to be alone.

Mme. Mercadet (aside)

Is he going to hatch some plot against his creditors? I must find out.

Come, Julie.

Julie

Papa, how good you are!

Mercadet

Nonsense!

Julie

I love you so much.

Mercadet

Nonsense!

Julie

Adolphe, I do not thank you, I shall have all my life for that.

Minard

Dearest Julie!

Mercadet (leading them out) Come, now, you had better breathe out your idyls in some more retired spot.

(They go out.)

SCENE THIRD

Mercadet, then De la Brive.

Mercadet I have resisted—it was a good impulse! But I was wrong to obey it. If I finally yield to the temptation, I can make their little capital worth very much more. I shall manage this fortune for them. My poor daughter has indeed a good lover. What hearts of gold are theirs! Dear children! (Goes towards the door at the right.) I must make their fortune. De la Brive is here awaiting me. (Looking through the open door) I believe he is asleep. I gave him a little too much wine, so as to handle him more easily. (Shouting) Michonnin! The constable! The constable!

De la Brive (coming out, rubbing his eyes)

Hello! What are you saying?

Mercadet Don't be frightened, I only wanted to wake you up. (Takes his seat at the table.)

De la Brive (sitting at the other side of the table) Sir, an orgie acts on the mind like a storm on the country. It brings on refreshment, it clothes with verdure! And ideas spring forth and bloom! /In vino varietas/!

Mercadet

Yesterday, our conversation on business matters was interrupted.

De la Brive Father-in-law, I recall it distinctly—we recognized the fact that our houses could not keep their engagements. We were on the point of bankruptcy, and you are unfortunate enough to be my creditor, while I am fortunate enough to be your debtor by the amount of forty-seven thousand, two hundred and thirty-three francs and some centimes.

Mercadet

Your head is level enough.

De la Brive But my pocket and my conscience are a little out. Yet who can reproach me? By squandering my fortune I have brought profit to every trade in Paris, and even to those who do not know me. We, the useless ones! We, the idlers! Upon my soul! It is we who keep up the circulation of money—

Mercadet By means of the money in circulation. Ah! you have all your wits about you!

De la Brive

But I have nothing else.

Mercadet Our wits are our mint. Is it not so? But, considering your present situation, I shall be brief.

De la Brive

That is why I take a seat.

Mercadet Listen to me. I see that you are going down the steep way which leads to that daring cleverness for which fools blame successful operators. You have tasted the piquant intoxicating fruits of Parisian pleasure. You have made luxury the inseparable companion of your life. Paris begins at the Place de l'Etoile, and ends at the Jockey Club. That is your Paris, which is the world of women who are talked about too much, or not at all.

De la Brive

That is true.

Mercadet You breathe the cynical atmosphere of wits and journalists, the atmosphere of the theatre and of the ministry. It is a vast sea in which thousands are casting their nets! You must either continue this existence, or blow your brains out!

De la Brive

No! For it is impossible to think that it can continue without me.

Mercadet Do you feel that you have the genius to maintain yourself in style at the height to which you aspire? To dominate men of mind by the power of capital and superiority of intellect? Do you think that you will always have skill enough to keep afloat between the two capes, which have seen the life of elegance so often founder between the cheap restaurant and the debtors' prison?

De la Brive Why! You are breaking into my conscience like a burglar—you echo my very thought! What do you want with me?

Mercadet

I wish to rescue you, by launching you into the world of business.

De la Brive

By what entrance?

Mercadet

Let me choose the door.

De la Brive

The devil!

Mercadet

Show yourself a man who will compromise himself for me—

De la Brive

But men of straw may be burnt.

Mercadet

You must be incombustible.

De la Brive

What are the terms of our copartnership?

Mercadet You try to serve me in the desperate circumstances in which I am at present, and I will make you a present of your forty-seven thousand, two hundred and thirty-three francs, to say nothing of the centimes. Between ourselves, I may say that only address is needed.

De la Brive

In the use of the pistol or the sword?

Mercadet

No one is to be killed; on the contrary—

De la Brive

That will suit me.

Mercadet

A man is to be brought to life again.

De la Brive That doesn't suit me at all, my dear fellow. The legacy, the chest of Harpagon, the little mule of Scapin and, indeed, all the farces which have made us laugh on the ancient stage are not well received nowadays in real life. The police have a way of getting mixed up with them, and since the abolition of privileges, no one can administer a drubbing with impunity.

Mercadet Well, what do you think of five years in debtors' prison? Eh? What a fate!

De la Brive As a matter of fact, my decision must depend upon what you want me to do to any one, for my honor so far is intact and is worth—

Mercadet You must invest it well, for we shall have dire need of all that it is worth. I want you to assist me in sitting at the table which the

Exchange always keeps spread, and we will gorge ourselves with the good things there offered us, for you must admit that while those who seek for millions have great difficulty in finding them, they are never found by those who do not seek.

De la Brive I think I can co-operate with you in this matter. You will return to me my forty-seven thousand francs—

Mercadet

Yes, sir.

De la Brive

I am not required to be anything but be—very clever?

Mercadet Nimble, but this nimbleness will be exercised, as the English say, on the right side of the law.

De la Brive

What is it you propose?

Mercadet (giving him a paper) Here are your written instructions. You are to represent something like an uncle from America—in fact, my partner, who has just come back from the West Indies.

De la Brive

I understand.

Mercadet Go to the Champs-Elysees, secure a post-chaise that has been much battered, have horses harnessed to it, and make your arrival here wrapped in a great pelisse, your head enveloped in a huge cap, while you shiver like a man who finds our summer icy cold. I will receive you; I will conduct you in; you will speak to my creditors; not one of them knows Godeau; you will make them give me more time.

De la Brive

How much time?

Mercadet I need only two days—two days, in order that Pierquin may complete certain purchases which we have ordered. Two days in order that the stock which I know how to inflate may have time to rise. You will be my backer, my security. And as no one will recognize you—

De la Brive I shall cease to be this personage as soon as I have paid you forty- seven thousand, two hundred and thirty-three francs and some centimes.

Mercadet

That is so. But I hear some one—my wife—

Mme. Mercadet (enters) My dear, there are some letters for you, and the bearer requires an answer.

(Mme. Mercadet withdraws to the fireplace.)

Mercadet

I suppose I must go. Good-day, my dear De la Brive. (In a low voice) Not a word to my wife; she would not understand the operation, and would misconstrue it. (Aloud) Go quickly, and forget nothing.

De la Brive

You need have no fear.

(Mercadet goes out by the left; De la Brive starts to go out by the centre, but Mme. Mercadet intercepts him.)

SCENE FOURTH

Mme. Mercadet and De la Brive.

De la Brive

Madame?

Mme. Mercadet

Forgive me, sir!

De la Brive

Kindly excuse me, madame, I must be going—

Mme. Mercadet

You must not go.

De la Brive

But you are not aware—

Mme. Mercadet

I know all.

De la Brive

How is that?

Mme. Mercadet You and my husband are bent upon resorting to some very ancient expedients proper to the comic drama, and I have employed one which is more ancient still. And as I told you, I know all—

De la Brive (aside)

She must have been listening.

Mme. Mercadet Sir, the part which you have been induced to undertake is blameworthy and shameful, and you must give it up—

De la Brive

But after all, madame—

Mme. Mercadet Oh! I know to whom I am speaking, sir; it was only a few hours ago that I saw you for the first time, and yet—I think I know you.

De la Brive

Really? I am sure I do not know what opinion you have of me.

Mme. Mercadet One day has given me time to form a correct judgment of you—and at the very time that my husband was trying to discover some foible in you he might make use of, or what evil passions he might rouse in you, I looked in your heart and discerned that it still contained good feelings which eventually may prove your salvation.

De la Brive

Prove my salvation? Excuse me, madame.

Mme. Mercadet Yes, sir, prove your salvation and that of my husband; for both of you are on the way to ruin. For you must understand that debts are no disgrace to any one who admits them and toils for their payment. You have your whole life before you, and you have too much good sense to wish that it should be blighted through engaging in a business which justice is sure to punish.

De la Brive Justice! Ah! You are right, madame, and I certainly would not lend myself to this dangerous comedy, unless your husband had some notes of hand of mine—

Mme. Mercadet

Which he will surrender to you, sir, I'll promise you that.

De la Brive

But, madame, I cannot pay them—

Mme. Mercadet We will be satisfied with your word, and you will discharge your obligation as soon as you have honestly made your fortune.

De la Brive

Honestly! That will be perhaps a long time to wait.

Mme. Mercadet

We will be patient. And now, sir, go and inform my husband that he must give up this attempt because he will not have your co-operation.

(She goes towards the door on the left.)

De la Brive I should be rather afraid to face him— I should prefer to write to him.

Mme. Mercadet (pointing out to him the door by which he entered) You will find the necessary writing materials in that room. Remain there until I come for your letter. I will hand it to him myself.

De la Brive I will do so, madame. After all I am not so worthless as I thought I was. It is you who have taught me this; you have a right to the whole credit of it. (He respectfully kisses her hand.) Thank you, madame, thank you! (He goes out.)

Mme. Mercadet

I have succeeded—if only I could now persuade Mercadet.

Justin (entering from the center)

Madame—madame—here they are—all of them.

Mme. Mercadet

Who?

Justin

The creditors.

Mme. Mercadet

Already?

Justin

There are a great many of them, madame.

Mme. Mercadet

Let them come in here. I will go and inform my husband.

(Mme. Mercadet goes out by one door. Justin opens the other.)

SCENE FIFTH

Pierquin, Goulard, Violette and several other creditors.

Goulard

Gentlemen, we have quite made up our minds, have we not?

All

We have, we have—

Pierquin

No more deluding promises.

Goulard

No more prayers and expostulations.

Violette No more pretended payments on account, thrown out as a bait to get deeper into our pockets.

SCENE SIXTH

The same persons and Mercadet.

Mercadet And do you mean to tell me that you gentlemen are come to force me into bankruptcy?

Goulard

We shall do so, unless you find means to pay us in full this very day.

Mercadet

To-day!

Pierquin

This very day.

Mercadet (standing before the fireplace) Do you think that I possess the plates for striking off Bank of France notes?

Violette

You mean that you have no offer to make?

Mercadet Absolutely none! And you are going to lock me up? I warn him who is going to pay for the cab that he won't be reimbursed from any assets of mine.

Goulard I shall add that along with all that you owe me to the debit of your account—

Mercadet

Thank you. You've all made up your mind, I suppose?

The Creditors

We have.

Mercadet I am touched by your unanimity! (pulling out his watch) Two o'clock. (Aside) De la Brive has had quite time enough—he ought to be on his way here. (Aloud) Gentlemen, you compel me to admit that you are men of inspiration and have chosen your time well!

Pierquin

What does he mean?

Mercadet For months, for years, you have allowed yourselves to be humbugged by fine promises, and deceived—yes, deceived by preposterous stories; and to-day is the day you choose for showing yourselves inexorable! Upon my word and honor, it is positively amusing! By all means let us start for Clichy.

Goulard

But, sir—

Pierquin

He is laughing.

Violette (rising from his chair) There is something in the wind. Gentlemen, there is something in the wind!

Pierquin

Please explain to us—

Goulard

We desire to know—

Violette (rising to his feet)

M. Mercadet, if there is anything—tell us about it.

Mercadet (coming to the table) Nothing! I shall say nothing, not I—I wish to be put behind the bars!—I would like to see the figure you all will cut to-morrow or this evening, when you find he has returned.

Goulard (rising to his feet)

He has returned?

Pierquin

Returned from where?

Violette

Who has returned?

Mercadet (coming forward)

Nobody has returned. Let us start for Clichy, gentlemen.

Goulard

But listen, if you are expecting any assistance—

Pierquin

If you have any hope that—

Violette

Or if even some considerable legacy—

Goulard

Come, now!

Pierquin

Answer—

Violette

Tell us—

Mercadet Now, take care, I beg you. You are giving way, you are giving way, gentlemen, and if I wished to take the trouble, I could win you over again. Come now, act like genuine creditors! Ridicule the past, forget the brilliant strokes of business I put within the power of each of you before the sudden departure of my faithful Godeau—

Goulard

His faithful Godeau!

Pierquin

Ah! If there were only—

Mercadet Forget all that preposterous past, take no account of what might induce him to return—after being waited for so long—and—let us start for Clichy, gentlemen, let us start for Clichy!

Violette

Mercadet, you are expecting Godeau, aren't you?

Mercadet

No!

Violette (as with a sudden inspiration)

Gentlemen, he is expecting Godeau!

Goulard

Can it be true?

Pierquin

Speak.

All

Speak! Speak!

Mercadet (with feeble deprecations) Why, no, no—yet I do not know—I— Certainly, it is possible that some day or other he may return form the Indies with some— considerable fortune— (In a decided tone) But I give you my word of honor that I don't expect Godeau here to-day.

Violette (excitedly)

Then it must be to-morrow! Gentlemen, he expects him to-morrow!

Goulard (in a low voice to the others)

Unless this is some fresh trick to gain time and ridicule us—

Pierquin (aloud)

Do you think it might be?

Goulard

It is quite possible.

Violette (in a loud tone)

Gentlemen, he is fooling us.

Mercadet (aside)

The devil he is! (Aloud) Come, gentlemen, we had better be starting.

Goulard

I swear that—

(The rumbling of carriage wheels is heard.)

Mercadet (aside)

At last! (Aloud) Oh, heavens! (He lays his hand upon his heart.)

A Postillion (outside)

A carriage at the door.

Mercadet

Ah! (Falls back on a chair near the table.)

Goulard (looking through the pane of glass above the mantel)

A carriage!

Pierquin (doing the same)

A post-chaise!

Violette (doing the same)

Gentlemen, a post-chaise is at the door.

Mercadet (aside)

My dear De la Brive could not have arrived at a better moment!

Goulard

See how dusty it is!

Violette

And battered to the very hood! It must have come from the heart of the Indies, to be as battered as that.

Mercadet (mildly) You don't know what you are talking about, Violette! Why, my good fellow, people don't arrive from the Indies by land.

Goulard

But come and see for yourself, Mercadet; a man has stepped out—

Pierquin

Enveloped in a large pelisse—do come—

Mercadet

No—pardon me. The joy—the excitement—I—

Violette He carries a chest. Oh! what a huge chest! Gentlemen, it is Godeau! I recognize him by the chest.

Mercadet

Yes—I was expecting Godeau.

Goulard

He has come back from Calcutta.

Pierquin

With a fortune.

Mercadet

Of incalculable extent!

Violette

What have I been saying?

(Violette goes in silence to Mercadet and grasps his hand. The two others follow his example, and then all the creditors form a ring round Mercadet.)

Mercadet (with seeming emotion)

Oh! Gentlemen—my friends—my dear comrades—my children!

SCENE SEVENTH

The same persons and Mme. Mercadet.

Mme. Mercadet (entering from the left)

Mercadet! My dear!

Mercadet (aside) It is my wife. I thought that she had gone out. She is going to ruin everything!

Mme. Mercadet

My dear! I see that you don't know what has happened?

Mercadet

I? No, I don't—if I—

Mme. Mercadet

Godeau is returned.

Mercadet

Ah! You say? (Aside) I wonder if she suspects—

Mme. Mercadet

I have seen him—I have spoken to him. It was I who saw him first.

Mercadet (aside) De la Brive has won her over! What a man he is! (To Mme. Mercadet, low) Good, my dear wife, good! You will be our salvation.

Mme. Mercadet

But you don't understand me, it is really he, it is—

Mercadet (in a low voice)

Hush! (Aloud) I must—gentlemen—I must go and welcome him.

Mme. Mercadet No—wait, wait a little, my dear; poor Godeau has overtaxed his strength—scarcely had he reached my apartment when fatigue, excitement and a nervous attack overcame him—

Mercadet

Really! (Aside) How well she does it!

Violette

Poor Godeau!

Mme. Mercadet "Madame," he said to me, "go and see your husband. Bring me back his pardon; I do not wish to see him face to face, until I have repaired the past."

Goulard

That was fine.

Pierquin

It was sublime.

Violette

It melts me to tears, gentlemen, it melts me to tears.

Mercadet (aside) Look at that! Well! There's a woman worth calling a wife! (Taking her by the hand) My darling— Excuse me, gentlemen. (He kisses her on both cheeks. In a low voice) Things are going on finely.

Mme. Mercadet (in a low voice) How lucky this is, my dear! Better than anything you could have fancied.

Mercadet I should think so. (Aside) It is very much better. (Aloud) Go and look after him, my dear. And you, gentlemen, be good enough to pass into my office. (He points to the left.) Wait there till we settle our accounts.

(Mme. Mercadet goes out.)

Goulard

I am at your service, my friend—

Pierquin

Our excellent friend.

Violette

Friend, we are at your service.

Mercadet (supporting himself half-dazed against the table)

What do you think? And people said that I was nothing but a sharper!

Goulard

You! You are one of the most capable men in Paris.

Pierquin

Who is bound to make a million—as soon as he has a—

Violette

Dear M. Mercadet, we will give you as much time as you want.

All

Certainly.

Mercadet

This is a little late—but gentlemen, I thank you as heartily as if you had said it yesterday morning. Good-day. (In a low voice to Goulard) Within an hour your stock shall be sold—

Goulard

Good!

Mercadet (in a low voice to Pierquin)

Stay where you are.

(All the others enter the office.)

Pierquin

What can I do for you?

SCENE EIGHTH

Mercadet and Pierquin.

Mercadet We are now alone. There is no time to lose. The stock of Basse-Indre went down yesterday. Go to the Exchange, buy up two hundred, three hundred, four hundred—Goulard will deliver them to you—

Pierquin

And for what date, and on what collateral?

Mercadet Collateral? Nonsense! This is a cash deal; bring them to me to-day, and I will pay to-morrow.

Pierquin

To-morrow?

Mercadet

To-morrow the stock will have risen.

Pierquin

I suppose, considering your situation, that you are buying for Godeau.

Mercadet

Do you think so?

Pierquin

I presume he gave his orders in the letter which announced his return.

Mercadet Possibly so. Ah! Master Pierquin, we are going to take a hand in business again, and I guess that you will gain from this to the end of the year something like a hundred thousand francs in brokerage from us.

Pierquin

A hundred thousand francs!

Mercadet Let the stock be depressed below par, and then buy it in, and—(handing him a letter) see that this letter appears in the evening paper. This evening, at Tortoni's, you will see an immediate rise in the quotations. Now be quick about this.

Pierquin

I will fly. Good-bye. (Exit.)

SCENE NINTH

Mercadet, then Justin.

Mercadet How well everything is going on, when we consider our recent complications! When Mahomet had three reliable friends (and it was hard to find them) the whole world was his! I have now won over as my allies all my creditors, thanks to the pretended arrival of Godeau. And I gain eight days, which means fifteen, with regard to actual payment. I shall buy three hundred thousand francs' worth of Basse-Indre before Verdelin. And when Verdelin asks for some of that stock, he will find it has risen, for a demand will have raised it above the current quotation, and I shall make at one stroke six hundred thousand francs. With three hundred thousand I will pay my creditors and show myself a Napoleon of finance. (He struts up and down.)

Justin (from the back of the stage)

Sir—

Mercadet

What is it—what do you want, Justin?

Justin

Sir—

Mercadet

Go on! Tell me.

Justin

M. Violette has offered me sixty francs if I will let him speak with M. Godeau.

Mercadet

Sixty francs. (Aside) He fleeced me out of them.

Justin

I am sure, sir, that you wouldn't like me to lose such a present.

Mercadet

Let him have his way with you.

Justin

Ah! sir, but—M. Goulard also—and the others—

Mercadet

Do as you like—I give them over into your hands. Fleece them well!

Justin

I'll do my best. Thank you, sir.

Mercadet

Let them all see Godeau. (Aside) De la Brive is well able to look after himself. (Aloud) But, between ourselves, keep Pierquin away. (Aside) He would recognize his dear friend, Michonnin.

Justin

I understand, sir. Ah! here is M. Minard. (Exit.)

SCENE TENTH

Mercadet and Minard.

Minard (coming forward)

Ah, sir!

Mercadet

Well, M. Minard, and what brings you here?

Minard

Despair.

Mercadet

Despair?

Minard

M. Godeau has come back; and they say that you are now a millionaire!

Mercadet

Is that the cause of your despair?

Minard

Yes, sir.

Mercadet Well, you are a strange fellow! I disclose to you the fact of my ruin and you are delighted. You learn that good fortune has returned to me and you are overwhelmed with despair! And all the while you wish to enter into my family! Yet you act like my enemy—

Minard It is just my love that makes your good fortune so alarming to me; I fear all the while that you will now refuse me the hand—

Mercadet Of Julie? My dear Adolphe, all men of business have not put their heart in their money-bags. Our sentiments are not always to be reckoned by debit and credit. You offered me the thirty thousand francs that you possessed—I certainly have no right to reject you on account of certain millions. (Aside) Which I do not possess!

Minard

You bring back life to me.

Mercadet Well, I suppose that is true, but so much the better, for I am very fond of you. You are simple, honorable. I am touched, I am delighted. I am even charmed. Ah! Let me once get hold of my six hundred thousand francs and—(Sees Pierquin enter) Here they come—

SCENE ELEVENTH

The same persons, Pierquin and Verdelin.

Mercadet (leading Pierquin to the front of the stage without perceiving Verdelin)

Is it all right?

Pierquin (in some embarrassment)

It is all right. The stock is ours.

Mercadet (joyfully)

Bravo!

Verdelin (approaching Mercadet)

Good-day!

Mercadet

What! Verdelin —

Verdelin I find out that you have bought the stock before me, and that now I shall have to pay very much higher than I expected; but it is all right, it was well managed, and I am compelled to cry, "Hail to the King of the Exchange, Hail to the Napoleon of Finance!" (He laughs derisively.)

Mercadet (somewhat abashed)

What does he mean?

Verdelin

I'm only repeating what you said yesterday —

Mercadet

What I said?

Pierquin

The fact of it is, Verdelin does not believe in the return of Godeau —

Minard

Ah, sir!

Mercadet

Is there any doubt about it?

Verdelin (ironically) Doubt about it! There is more than doubt about it. I at once concluded that this so-called return was the bold stroke that you spoke of yesterday.

Mercadet

I—(Aside) Stupid of me!

Verdelin I concluded that, relying upon the presence of this fictitious Godeau, you made purchases with the idea of paying on the rise, which would follow to-morrow, and that to-day you have actually not a single sou—

Mercadet

You had imagined all that?

Verdelin (approaching the fireplace) Yes, but when I saw outside that triumphal post-chaise—that model of Indian manufacture, and I realized that it was impossible to find such a vehicle in the Champs-Elysees, all my doubts disappeared and— But hand him over the bonds, M. Pierquin!

Pierquin

The—bonds—it happens that—

Mercadet (aside)

I must bluff, or I am lost! (Aloud) Certainly, produce the bonds.

Pierquin

One moment—if what this gentleman has said is true—

Mercadet (haughtily)

M. Pierquin!

Minard But, gentlemen—M. Godeau is here—I have seen him—I have talked with him.

Mercadet (to Pierquin)

He has talked with him, sir.

Pierquin (to Verdelin)

The fact of it is, I have seen him myself.

Verdelin I don't doubt it! By the bye, on what vessel did our friend Godeau say he arrived?

Mercadet

By what vessel? It was by the—by the /Triton/—

Verdelin How careless the English newspapers are. They have published the arrival of no other English mail packet but the /Halcyon/.

Pierquin

Really!

Mercadet

Let us end this discussion. M. Pierquin—those bonds—

Pierquin Pardon me, but as you have offered no collateral, I would wish—I do wish to speak with Godeau.

Mercadet You shall not speak with him, sir. I cannot permit you to doubt my word.

Verdelin

This is superb.

Mercadet M. Minard, go to Godeau— Tell him that I have obtained an option on three hundred thousand francs' worth of stock, and ask him to send me —(with emphasis)—thirty thousand francs for use as a margin. A man in his position always has such a sum about him. (In a low voice) Do not fail to bring me the thirty thousand.

Minard

Yes, sir. (Goes out, through the right.)

Mercadet (haughtily)

Will that satisfy you, M. Pierquin?

Pierquin Certainly, certainly. (To Verdelin) It will be all right when he comes back.

Verdelin (rising from his seat)

And you expect that he will bring thirty thousand francs?

Mercadet I have a perfect right to be offended by your insulting doubt; but I am still your debtor—

Verdelin Bosh! You have enough in Godeau's pocket-book wherewith to liquidate; besides, to-morrow the Basse-Indre will rise above par. It will go up, up, till you don't know how far it will go. Your letter worked wonders, and we were obliged to publish on the Exchange the results of our explorations by boring. The mines will become as valuable as those of Mons—and—your fortune is made—when I thought I was going to make mine.

Mercadet I now understand your rage. (To Pierquin) And this is the origin of all the doubtful rumors.

Verdelin

Rumors which can only vanish before the appearance of Godeau's cash.

SCENE TWELFTH

The same persons, Violette and Goulard.

Goulard

Ah! my friend!

Violette (following him)

My dear Mercadet!

Goulard

What a man this Godeau is!

Mercadet (aside)

Fine!

Violette

What high sense of honor he has!

Mercadet (aside)

That's pretty good!

Goulard

What magnanimity!

Mercadet (aside)

Prodigious!

Verdelin

Have you seen him?

Violette

Of course, I have!

Pierquin

Have you spoken to him?

Goulard

Just as I speak to you. And I have been paid.

All

Paid!

Mercadet

Paid? How—how have you been paid?

Goulard

In full. Fifty thousand in drafts.

Mercadet (aside)

That I can understand.

Goulard

And eight thousand francs net, in notes.

Mercadet

In bank-notes?

Goulard

Bank-notes.

Mercadet (aside) It is past my understanding. Ah! Eight thousand! Minard might have given them, so that now he'll bring me only twenty-two thousand.

Violette And I—I, who would have been willing to make some reduction—I have been paid in full!

Mercadet

All! (in a low voice to him) I suppose in drafts?

Violette

In first-class drafts to the amount of eighteen thousand francs.

Mercadet (aside)

What a fellow this De la Brive is!

Violette

And the balance, the other twelve thousand—

Verdelin

Yes—the balance?

Violette

In cash. Here it is. (He shows the bank-notes.)

Mercadet (aside)

Minard won't bring me more than ten.

Goulard (taking a seat at the table)

And this very moment he is paying in the same way all your creditors.

Mercadet

In the same way?

Violette (taking a seat at the table)

Yes, in drafts, in specie, and in bank-notes.

Mercadet (forgetting himself)

Lord, have mercy upon me! (Aside) Minard will bring me nothing at all.

Verdelin

What is the matter with you?

Mercadet

Me! Nothing—I—

SCENE THIRTEENTH

The same persons and Minard, followed by creditors.

Minard

I have done your errand.

Mercadet (trembling)

And you—have brought me—a few—bank-notes?

Minard A few bank-notes? Of course. M. Godeau wouldn't let me even mention the thirty thousand francs.

(Goulard and Violette rise. Minard stands before the table, surrounded by creditors.)

Mercadet

I can quite understand that.

Minard "You mean," he said, "a hundred thousand crowns; here are a hundred thousand crowns, with my compliments!" (He pulls out a large roll of bank-notes, which he places on the table.)

Mercadet (rushing to the table)

What the devil! (Looking at the notes) What is all this about?

Minard

The three hundred thousand francs.

Pierquin

My three hundred thousand francs!

Verdelin

The truth for once!

Mercadet (astounded)

Three hundred thousand francs! I see them! I touch them! I grasp them! Three hundred thousand—where did you get them?

Minard

I told you he gave them to me.

Mercadet (with vehemence)

He!— He—! Who is he?

Minard

Did not I say, M. Godeau?

Mercadet

What Godeau? Which Godeau?

Minard

Why the Godeau who has come back from the Indies.

Mercadet

From the Indies?

Violette

And who is paying all your debts.

Mercadet

What is this? I never expected to strike a Godeau of this kind.

Pierquin

He has gone crazy!

(All the other creditors gather at the back of the stage. Verdelin approaches them, and speaks in a low voice.)

Verdelin (returning to Mercadet)

It's true enough! All are paid in full!

Mercadet Paid? Every one of them? (Goes from one to the other and looks at the bank-notes and the drafts they have.) Yes, all settled with—settled in full! Ah! I see blue, red, violet! A rainbow seems to surround me.

SCENE FOURTEENTH

The same persons, Mme. Mercadet, Julie (entering at one side) and De la Brive (entering at the other side).

Mme. Mercadet

My friend, M. Godeau, feels himself strong enough to see you all.

Mercadet Come, daughter, wife, Adolphe, and my other friends, gather round me, look at me. I know you would not deceive me.

Julie

What is the matter, father?

Mercadet

Tell me (seeing De la Brive come in) Michonnin, tell me frankly—

De la Brive Luckily for me, sir, I followed the advice of madame—otherwise you would have had two Godeaus at a time, for heaven has brought back to you the genuine man.

Mercadet

You mean to say then—that he has really returned!

Verdelin

Do you mean to say that you didn't know it after all?

Mercadet (recovering himself, standing before the table and touching the notes) I—of course I did. Oh, fortune, all hail to thee, queen of monarchs, archduchess of loans, princess of stocks and mother of credit! All hail! Thou long sought for, and now for the thousandth time come home to us from the Indies! Oh! I've always said that Godeau had a mind of tireless energy and an honest heart! (Going up to his wife and daughter) Kiss me!

Mme. Mercadet (in tears)

Ah! dear, dear husband!

Mercadet (supporting her)

And you, what courage you have shown in adversity!

Mme. Mercadet

But I am overcome by the happiness of seeing you saved—wealthy!

Mercadet But honest! And yet I must tell you my wife, my children—I could not have held out much longer—I was about to succumb—my mind always on the rack—always on the defensive—a giant might have yielded. There were moments when I longed to flee away— Oh! For some place of repose! Henceforth let us live in the country.

Mme. Mercadet

But you will soon grow weary of it.

Mercadet No, for I shall be a witness in their happiness. (Pointing to Minard and Julie.) And after all this financial traffic I shall devote myself to agriculture; the study of agriculture will never prove tedious. (To the creditors) Gentlemen, we will continue to be good friends, but will have no more business transactions. (To De la Brive) M. de la Brive, let me pay back to you your forty-eight thousand francs.

De la Brive

Ah! sir—

Mercadet

And I will lend you ten thousand more.

De la Brive

Ten thousand francs? But I don't know when I shall be able—

Mercadet

You need have no scruples; take them—for I have a scheme—

De la Brive

I accept them.

Mercadet Ah! It is one of my dreams. Gentlemen (to the creditors who are standing in a row) I am a—creditor!

Mme. Mercadet (pointing to the door)

My dear, he is waiting for us.

Mercadet

Yes, let us go in. I have so many times drawn your attention to Godeau, that I certainly have the right to see him. Let us go in and see Godeau!

Final curtain.